Speechmakers' Bible

Speechmakers' Bible

First published in the UK in 1997 by Ward Lock as
The Complete Speechmaker

This revised and updated edition published in 2006 by
Cassell Illustrated
A division of Octopus Publishing Group Ltd
2–4 Heron Quays
London E14 4JP

Speechmakers' Bible has been compiled from
Jokes and Quotes for Speeches by Peter Eldin
Wedding Speeches and Toasts by Angela Lansbury
Speeches and Presentations by Jane Willis
(for further information visit her website
www.Speakwellcommunications.co.uk) and revised
and updated by Nick Marshallsay and Jane Moseley.

A CIP catalogue record for this book is available
from the British Library.

ISBN-13: 978-1-844033-37-9
ISBN-10: 1-844033-37-6

Printed in Italy

contents

Introduction

'You'll have to make a speech!' are words you may wish never to hear. It may be for a wedding, a business lunch`, an informal group, the Parent-teacher Association, a school speech day, or an informal family celebration. But have no fear. Whatever your experience, and despite what you may think, speechmaking can be fun and this book is here to help you.

There are two principal factors involved in the making of a public speaker: there is the person who makes and delivers the speech, and there is the message that the speaker delivers. Some people are naturally more extrovert than others and thrive on audience attention, while others shy away from it and may remember stumbling over a passage they had to read aloud in school This book will guide you through preparing yourself for standing up in front of both small and large groups of people, and for preparing any material you may need to use if you are giving a business presentation or a talk to a local society.

There are tips and hints on making yourself feel at ease with the situation and on coping with nerves, breathing and voice control exercises, advice on body language, and even suggestions on the type of clothing you should and shouldn't wear. The actual writing of the speech may seem daunting but *Speechmakers' Bible* will guide you from your first word to your concluding statement.

One of the problems in giving a speech is finding appropriate jokes and quotes to include. To help with this there are two extensive reference sections which are in subject order and many of the suggestions can be adapted for other situations. If you are searching for material for a wedding speech, for example, do not just refer to the section on weddings and anniversaries. Suitable material will also be found in the section on birthdays. More general jokes and quotes are worth considering for any type of speech, as even areas that have nothing to do with your subject may provide the spark that will lift your speech from predictable run-of-the-mill to something your audience will remember for a long time to come.

Although the general sections of this book will be of use to all, whatever type of speech or presentation being planned, those of you who have been asked to talk at a wedding or celebrations will find more advice in Chapter Seven. If you are embarking on a business presentation, refer to Chapter Six for specific ideas and suggestions, and guidelines on the use of audio-visual material. Advice for after-dinner speakers can also be found in Chapter Six and those finding themselves with the challenge of chairing a meeting should look for the guidance given in Chapter Six.

'You'll have to make a speech!' – and with the help of this book you'll not only have the confidence to do this but you might even enjoy it as well!

speechmakers' bible

chapter 1

Preparing
yourself

No peak performer would ever consider going into a high-stakes situation ill-prepared: Tiger Woods would never enter a tournament without having perfected his shots, a musician without having had rehearsals, or an actor without having practised their lines. In the same way, a cornerstone of effective speechmaking is preparing yourself to be at the top of your game. In this chapter we will look at coping with nerves, exercising our voices to have maximum impact, and limbering up our language skills to articulate clear and well-thought out messages. Like the marathon runner who knows they have put in the hard training miles, when we take to the stage we will have the confidence of knowing we have done the work required to deliver a fantastic speech.

The better prepared you are in advance the less agitated and unsure you will feel when the day of your speech arrives. Use every opportunity to listen and watch other good speakers. Notice the way they construct and deliver their sentences. The more direct and simple the message, the more readily it is communicated. Shorter sentences hold impact and are easier to grasp than long ones. They also help to discipline the speaker from straying off the point.

Coping with nerves

Tell yourself that you are looking forward to your speech. Keep saying this to yourself until you believe it. When you finally stand in front of the audience, say to yourself: 'I'm glad to be here. I wish this to go well.' This reinforces feelings of goodwill and will express itself through your body language and voice.

TOP TIPS TO DEAL WITH NERVES

Rehearse: Nerves are often driven by fear and unfamiliarity. Rehearsal makes you familiar and comfortable with your content and environment.

Deep breaths: Nerves create shallow, rapid breathing. Regain control by breathing in slowly and deeply, holding for a count of three and then breathing out slowly.

Using an anecdote or 'engagement item': When people start presenting they often mechanically read from notes or visual aids, stumbling over their words, especially when they begin. Try starting instead by telling a relevant anecdote or story to get over the difficult first few lines (see Chapter Two).

Know your intro: Most speakers are at their most nervous at the beginning. By making the start almost second nature you'll ease comfortably into the main body of the speech or presentation.

You will always feel ten times more nervous than you look: *'You looked so confident up there.'* Little do they know the serene swan was paddling like mad below the surface. By giving the impression of confidence we often become confident. Stand with relaxed shoulders positioned behind the hips, anchor yourself gently to a chair or podium, smile and hold your head level looking at the audience...fake it and you'll rapidly make it!

Try the following exercises to help you relax:

EXERCISE 1
THE SHOULDERS

Standing in a relaxed position, lift the shoulders slightly and tense them. Now relax them by letting them fall. Note the difference. Sometimes we lift the shoulders and tense them without realizing that we are doing so. When the shoulders are tensed, the neck becomes tight and we can feel very uncomfortable and tire more easily.

EXERCISE 2
THE NECK

Imagine that you have a very long neck. It is perfectly posed between the shoulders, which are relaxed and down. Your chin tucks in naturally and with ease. Now move your head gently and, with a feeling of elegance, turn your head to the left. Next, gently turn your head from the left to the front. Pause. Now gently turn your head to the right and then to the front. Pause. Imagine being in front of an audience. Repeat the exercise, pretending you are sweeping your listeners with your eyes. Take it slowly and rhythmically, keeping in your mind a feeling of calmness and dignity.

EXERCISE 3
THE HEAD

Imagine that your head is made of granite. In a standing position, let the head slowly, very slowly, fall onto your chest. It feels so heavy that it must succumb to the force of gravity. Keep this feeling with you.

Now for the transformation! Your head is now as light as cotton wool as it floats to an upright position.

Practise this several times to experience the contrast between the feelings of lightness and heaviness.

EXERCISE 4
A GENTLE SIGH

Standing in a relaxed, upright position, inhale slowly and then emit a slow, gentle sigh of relief. Think of the sigh as though it were coming from the centre of your body. The shoulders should be down and relaxed. The feeling is one of letting go. As you inhale, place your hands on the lower ribs on either side of your waist and experience the gentle upward and lateral movement of these ribs.

EXERCISE 5
CONCENTRATION

Choose an object that appeals to you – an ornament or flower, perhaps. Sit in a chair with a well-supporting back, and place the object in front of you. Now fix your mind on it. Take in as much detail as you can: colour, texture, shape and so on. Concentrate, giving it your full attention. Now, resting your head against the back of the chair, close your eyes and place the image of that object in your mind. See if you can recall an accurate likeness. When you are ready, open your eyes.

EXERCISE 6
VISUALIZING AN ENTRANCE

Use your dining room table and chairs for this one.

Imagine that you are a guest speaker at a meeting or function. Around the table are seated business associates or wedding guests. Carry a folder (if you are imagining a business situation) or gloves (if this is a wedding scenario) and enter the room in a pessimistic manner. Eyes cast down perhaps, the walk uncertain, with rounded or tense shoulders. Walk to the table, place the folder/gloves on it and sit. All your movements suggest lack of confidence and assertiveness.

Repeat the exercise. Again, you are very tense and unhappy about the prospect of this meeting or wedding speech. But in this instance it is important that you are seen to be in charge of the situation. Your audience must not see how you feel.

You are on the defensive. The body is held stiffly. The shoulders are hunched. The face is set and unsmiling. The walk is stilted. You may cough nervously and play with your tie or necklace as you take a seat at the table. You reach over for a drink of water. Your hands are shaking. Visualize the effect this might have on the others.

You are now entering the room for the third time. On this occasion you are optimistic and positive. The shoulders are relaxed and down and the head is well balanced between the shoulder blades. The eyes sweep the table where the others are seated and they reflect warmth, interest and enthusiasm. Walking to your seat with purpose and drive, place the folder/gloves on the table. When seated, rest your arms on the table with hands lightly clasped. Smile pleasantly. It is a smile that has arisen from a knowledge that your feeling of self-esteem is high. It tells the others that you are pleased to be among them and are ready to entertain or do business.

EXERCISE 7
RECALLING A SPEECH

Sit in a chair and think about a speech that you have heard in the past. Recall the audience. How did they react to the talk? Did they appear happy and satisfied or bored and restless? Was the speaker attractive in appearance and manner? If so, why? How did he or she move? Was the voice interesting? Was the message communicated clear and concise? Were there amusing breaks, offering light relief?

Now imagine that it is you giving the speech in place of the speaker. It may be a similar talk, given to the same audience. How would you like to be seen? Try to see yourself through the eyes of that audience. Listen to their needs. Think it through stage by stage from the entrance, when you walk to the platform, or rise from your seat, to the applause at the end.

Breath and the voice

Breathing is a natural function that we don't often think about. However, paying it some attention is necessary for those who find it difficult to project their voices when speaking in public.

To be heard while addressing an audience, we need to create space in the throat and chest so that the right amount of air is directed through the vocal chords. The throat, mouth and nose help us to amplify our sound, which would be less audible if it did not pass through these. The mouth and throat should therefore be free of tension, and the nose kept clear and unblocked, in order for the resonators to function effectively. These exercises will help your breath control:

 **EXERCISE 8**
BREATHING IN

Stand straight but not stiffly. This is important, as good alignment will promote strong voice production. Remember when you inhale not to raise your shoulders. Doing so will encourage tension in the neck, throat and breathing muscles.

Now feel your ribcage. Ribs form the thorax and are attached at the back to the twelve thoracic vertebrae. Rest one hand on your midriff and the other on your lower ribs that reach round the waist. Breathe in slowly and notice how the hand resting on the midriff moves out slightly. This has happened because the diaphragm, which is a muscular partition that separates the thorax from the abdomen, has contracted and flattened, thereby pushing the belly outwards. Because the lower ribs are more flexible than those higher up, they will flex upwards and outwards by the use of the intercostal muscles that are attached to them.

This muscular activity expands the chest cavity, creating more space for the lungs to fill with air, which is drawn into them through the windpipe, nose and/or mouth.

EXERCISE 9
BREATHING OUT

Now breathe out slowly and feel the lower ribs gradually relax as the lungs contract, the diaphragm rises and the midriff or belly moves inwards. As this is happening, the transverse abdominal muscles are gently drawn inwards. This contraction of the abdominal muscles is used to help expel our outgoing breath when we speak, gently supporting the diaphragm and lower ribs, so that sound can be sustained and energized.

Remember: breath in, hand on midriff moves outwards; breath out, hand moves inwards.

Because it is on the outgoing breath that we speak, we aim to balance breath with sound. The moment we start to exhale, we need to use the voice. Aim to achieve this smoothness in the following exercise (Exercise 10). Practising regularly and for short periods should help give you the breath control that is needed when speaking in front of an audience.

Physical tensions and feelings of nervousness may be increased, or even caused by the insufficient intake of air; at times, this can result in a sore throat, breathy or strained voice and tailing off at the ends of sentences. Some speakers do not allow themselves breathing space! They take in small gasps of air and do not take advantage of their breathing muscles. The shoulders may rise on inhalation, which encourages the ribs to move in one way only – vertically – and this can constrict the breath. The ribs need to flex vertically and laterally. Raising the arms slightly to the side while practising breathing in may provide a picture of opening out, so that lateral expansion is encouraged.

EXERCISE 10
HUMMING

HUM. This is a very resonant sound. As you do this, be aware of the vibrations by touching your throat, lips and nose. Now, taking a full breath, increase the volume of the hum until quite loud. Stay relaxed, avoid strain, and rest in between exercises.

EXERCISE 11
HOORAH!

Take the word HOORAH! Repeat it several times with freedom and spontaneity. This is a valuable exercise as an aid for overcoming inhibitions. Use your arm to guide your sound forward and have fun with it!

EXERCISE 12
SOUND FROM YOUR CENTRE

Imagine the sound rising naturally from your midriff or centre as you speak the following sentences. Allow your thoughts to guide the sense of what you are saying. Remember to pause and breathe after each sentence.

I am relaxed and confident.
My neck is free of tension.
I am filling my body with energy.
I am releasing my sound into the room.
I shall be heard.

The power behind your voice

When speaking in public, the voice needs to be strong without straining or shouting. Your breath is the power behind your voice. Imagine a string of pearls. The string has to be long enough to support the pearls, but if that string is weak and breaks, the pearls will scatter all over the floor. So it is with the voice. The string is the breath and the pearls are the words. There must, therefore, be enough breath-power behind the voice to support the words, otherwise the air will run out and the voice will falter and fade. It is important to inhale as much air as necessary. The aim is to flow and we breathe where there are natural pauses in the text.

Learn where to punctuate your speech and phrase your words. Do not break your phrases or your speech will become jerky and the sense may be lost. Gauge where you are going to take:

- Your full-stop pauses (remember you will pause longer and take a fuller breath at your full-stop break).
- Your comma pauses and supplementary breaths.

Speak the following exercise. Use this sign / for a comma breath pause and // for a full-stop breath pause.

As you take your breaths during this exercise, imagine that they are dropping into the centre of your body, at the waist. Breathe out with the words, keeping the voice sustained all the while. To help you, rest a hand on your midriff as you do this.

Ensure that you are standing straight, but be at ease, especially around the top part of your body, the neck, throat and shoulders, which should be relaxed and down. Stand with legs slightly apart, the weight evenly distributed on both feet. Your head needs to be well balanced between the shoulder blades. The chin should not jut out or be pushed too far into the neck. If you were speaking to a fairly large audience you would need to speak a little slower and very clearly.

EXERCISE 13
PHRASING AND PAUSING 1: JERSEY

The state of Jersey is a part of the Channel Islands, / and is twelve miles from the coast of France. //

Physical features resemble a mixture of Normandy in France, / and the county of Wiltshire in England. //

The island is small: / nine miles by five, / and divided into twelve parishes. //

Villages are picturesque, / comprising stone-built farms and well-kept houses. //

Winding roads are flanked on either side by soft rolling countryside, / small sheltered bays and natural harbours. //

The chief industry is market gardening; / and it is on this island that the well-known Jersey cow is reared. //

French influence on Jersey is reflected in the names of the roads, / and of some farms and houses. //

Although Jersey is a self-run state, / having its own legislative assemblies and legal systems, / it still remains part of the British Isles. //

In 1941, / Jersey was invaded and occupied by the German forces, / who remained there until the end of the war in 1945. //

EXERCISE 14
PHRASING AND PAUSING 2: THE SECRETARY BIRD

The secretary bird is an African bird of prey. //

It gets its name from the crest of long feathers on top of its head, / which resemble old quill pens. //

The plumage is grey and white, / with black hindquarters and black and white bars on the tail. //

It stands four feet tall, / has very long legs and a two-foot long tail. //

Secretary birds feed mainly on insects, / lizards and small snakes. //

The nest is built of sticks and clay, / and is used over a period of a few years. //

The large eggs are laid in August. //

When they are hatched, / the young birds do not leave the nest for about five months. //

Although secretary birds are powerful fliers, / they spend a great deal of their time on the ground. //

EXERCISE 15
PHRASING AND PAUSING 3: THE JAY

Before practising the next exercise, mark where you are going to place your breath pauses. Some of the sentences are quite long and require good breath support.

The history and grandeur of England rests on one bird, the jay. If it were not for this creature, Henry VIII's navy could not have set sail to conquer and build the great British Empire. The jay is responsible for the propagation of the English oak as it is the only species that commonly plants acorns. Unlike the squirrel, it does not bite off the fruit's tip, and prevent germination.

There are more exercises to help you in developing ability to phrase and pause in Chapters Two and Four.

Using the muscles of the face

Exercises 16 and 17 will help to develop strong and flexible facial muscles.

Use a mirror to ensure that you are working the lip muscles. With the sound **w** as in **will**, bring the lips well forward into a small circle. For the **ee** sound as in the word **we**, gently draw the lips back as though you are giving someone a soft smile. Avoid overstretching the mouth as this will create tension, the very thing you need to avoid. Thorough but gentle exercise is what is needed and these exercises should be practised regularly prior to a public-speaking engagement.

EXERCISE 16
MOUTH AND LIP MUSCLES

Make a wide grin and then bring the lips forward into a pout.

Blow out through the lips like a baby.

Repeat the following:
Will we, will we, will we, wind down the window for Wilfred?
Wendy and Winifred, Wendy and Winifred.
Willy and Wendy and Winifred.

Next, mime the following poem by over-emphasizing the lip movements to gain full mobility of the mouth. This is important. Repeat using the voice. Speak it with expression and animation.

Weather talk
'Isn't it cold? Look at that rain!'
Stating the obvious time and again.
What should I answer?
'Yes, I can see!'
Really much easier to simply agree.

'Nicer today.' Nicer than what?
Oh, talk of the weather! (I almost forgot.)
'Yes, nicer indeed,'
I quickly assent
And almost as quickly I start to relent.

For what are you thinking?
Are you thinking as I –

'Don't talk of the weather,
Don't dwell on the sky.
Conventional, proper –
So socially right.
Much nicer to speak of the things that delight.'

Remember to use your mouth – you'll be clearer and understood. It is the consonants that provide the outline and cut to your words. No matter how well a person projects their voice, if the word endings are weak, they won't be heard or understood. So remember: clarity aids projection. In particular, watch for:

• T, d, m, n, l and k endings: e.g. tent, David, kick
• T, k, l, in the middle of words: e.g. butter, licking, illness

Lazy tongues make lazy speech

While consonants give clarity and cut to a word, vowels give tonal quality to the voice. Because this book is not an elocution manual, the formation of vowels and consonants will not be dealt with in intricate detail. Suffice to say that a consonant is formed by air coming from the larynx that is stopped by one or two of the articulate organs of speech – tongue, teeth, hard and soft palates, gums, lips – before it is released. For example, **d** requires that the vocalized breath from the larynx is stopped by the tongue-tip against the teeth ridge (the ridge formed behind the upper teeth), before being released as the sound **d. B** requires that the vocalized breath is stopped by the lips, before being released as the sound **b**. Other vocalized consonants are: **m, g, l, ge, n, ng, r, th, v, w,**

y and **z**. Some consonants use vocalized breath and some unvocalized, such as **k**. This requires unvocalized breath from the larynx being stopped by the back of the tongue arching towards the soft palate and then releasing. **P** is another unvocalized consonant, as are: **ch, f, h, sh, s, t** and **th**. These need particular care while enunciating. You will see that **th** appears in both lists, unvocalized as in: **Thursday, thanks, theatre** or vocalized as in: **this, that, there, those, than**.

Vowels, however, have a free, open passage. The lips and tongue shape the different sounds, but there is no truncation.

Make your consonants distinctly, and for the formation of the vowels, open your mouth to let out the sounds. Keep the jaw flexible. Imagine placing vowel sounds forward in the mouth – shaping the lips will help.

The following exercises use vowels and consonants. Aim for accurate and expressive delivery. Use generous mouth movements to exercise the muscles and help loosen the jaw. Avoid strain, as this can be counter-productive. Practise these exercises regularly prior to public-speaking engagements.

EXERCISE 17
LIP AND TONGUE WARM-UPS

Speak the following clearly and energetically. Aim for accuracy. When familiar with them, repeat with speed until you can speak them quickly without making a mistake. Use firm tongue and lip movements to exercise the muscles, but avoid strain.

- d d d t t t (Repeat 3 times)
- l l l k k k (Repeat 3 times)
- m m m n n n (Repeat 3 times)
- b b b p p p (Repeat 3 times)
- tot dod lel nell
- tok tuk tak tek
- lot lad led men
- bold helm land doubled
- better botter batter bitter
- heckle locker lacquer liquor
- meddled modelled middled troubled
- bep bap bip bop
- kep kap kip kop
- Stack the sacks and check the stock
- Double, double, toil and trouble
- Peter Piper picked a peck of pickled pepper

 EXERCISE 18
ARTICULATION FOR SHORT VOWELS PLUS CONSONANTS

- Angela is angry with Andy for antagonizing her Alsatian.
- Betty and Bill are Benny's best friends.
- Cats catch and kill canaries.
- Dennis and Dave drive dangerously down Dudden Hill.
- Eddie is extrovert, extravagant and entertaining.
- Flat fish and flying fish; fillet of fish and fish cakes.
- Ghastly Gordon greedily gobbles gherkins.
- Henry has a hundred hats hanging on his hat stand.
- Ingrid invites in-laws to Ipswich.

- Jolly Jasper jumps for joy.
- Kit eats Kit Kats in Kerry's kitchen.
- Lady Lavinia Luckham listens to Liszt.
- Mermaids' melodies are mesmerizing.
- Nattie's neighbours niggle noisily.
- Opulent Olive enjoys opera and oratorios.
- Pots, pans, powder and prunes.
- Quirky quacks quibble and quip.
- Running Richard races rogues round Rotten Row.
- Sally's sister Susie sambas.
- Trains, tickets and timetables are terribly trying.
- Uncle Ulric unfolds his umber umbrella.
- Puss chased the rooks by the brook in the wood.
- Vain Vinny varnishes vases with vivid violet.
- Wandering wenches wear wellingtons in wintry weather.
- Xavier's X-rays are excellent.
- Yokels yodel at Yuletide.
- Zig-zagging, zany zebras.

 **EXERCISE 19**
ARTICULATION FOR LONG VOWELS

ah   **Arnold, Jaguar, far, smarter, car, Carl, Ferrari**
Arnold's Jaguar is a far smarter car than Carl's Ferrari.

er   **early, bird, worm**
The early bird catches the worm.

aw   **wardrobes, warm, ward, hoary, storm**
Wardrobes must be warm, to ward off frost and storm.

oo   **goosey, soup, rooster, cook, mousse, noodle**
Goosey soup, rooster soup, cool mousse and noodle soup.

ee   **sleepy, dreamy, easy, stream**

Sleep, dreamy, take it easy; swim with the stream.

ew   **new, tulips, Duke, Tewkesbury**

The new tulips were given to the Duke when he visited Tewkesbury.

ay   **pale, maidens, bathe, daily, shady, glades**

Pale maidens bathe daily in the shady glades.

i   **nice, rice, light, white**

Nice rice, light rice, nice, white, light rice.

oy   **toys, boys**

Men with toys will always be boys.

ow   **brown, found, cow, lounge**

Mrs Brown found a cow in her front lounge.

oh   **Roland, wrote, odious, odes, Rhoda**

Roland wrote odious odes to Rhoda.

ear   **piercing, cheers, weary, ears**

Piercing cheers make weary ears.

air   **aeroplanes, heiresses, various, fair**

Aeroplanes fly heiresses to various fair places.

oor   **rural, tours, brochure**

Rural Tours are advertising their brochures.

ure   **Muriel, liqueur, ewer**

Muriel hides bottles of liqueur in the bathroom ewer.

ire   **choirs, lyres, friars**

Harmonizing choirs; lutes and lyres; monks and friars.

our   **flowers, showery, bowers**

Seeds burst into flowers in showery bowers.

Speaking with clarity

For the person who is a newcomer to public speaking, the task of channelling thoughts and setting them down on paper in an expressive fashion can be extremely difficult. The brain needs a prompt, some kind of stimulus to get it going in the direction for which it is intended. There needs to be a limbering-up period. Just as with keeping fit, the warming-up before exercise and the warming-down afterwards is considered essential in order to prevent undue stress on the body. And so exercises that encourage language skills can help fluency of speech.

The following exercises will encourage oral skills. They are meant to be fun and, like many games, you can play them singly, with a partner, or with members of your family. The exercises encourage imagination, accuracy and concentration. They all require self-involvement.

When practising these exercises, avoid over-use of the same word. For example, lovely. Alternatives might be: pleasing, elegant, graceful, fair, brilliant, radiant, etc. Choose vocabulary that enhances your descriptions. A thesaurus provides a wealth of adjectives that you can use. (There is more advice in Chapter Two on choosing words well.)

EXERCISE 20
VISUALIZATION

This exercise or game can be practised alone, with a partner, or within a group.

Sit back in a comfortable chair and close your eyes. Think back to a place you have visited. Maybe it was while on holiday; a cathedral, house or park. Take time to recall the place as accurately as you can. When you are ready, recount this memory aloud, either to yourself or to your partner. Having described the place, express your feelings about it. Why did you choose it? What was it that held special appeal for you? If at first you find this exercise difficult, start by describing some functional tasks, such as cooking breakfast, your journey to work, cleaning the car, etc. Focusing on detail can improve concentration skills – vital for public speaking.

If you are doing this exercise with a partner or group, take turns, and while one is recounting their scene, listen and concentrate to draw on your imagination to create as full a picture in your mind as possible of the speaker's account.

This exercise can be developed into story-telling. Choose a scene, such as a walk through the woods, or a visit to an art gallery. As before, sit with eyes closed and imagine yourself as a character within this scene. It can then be developed by the rest of the group. Centre your attention on the characters and the situations that evolve from them.

When the story is completed, write it down and read it aloud. Your thoughts and creative ideas have now become manifest. You have used your imaginative skills to formulate a story that has been processed from a memory or an idea. This has been expressed verbally, and then translated into the written word.

A similar development takes place when preparing a speech. You are given a theme or subject on which to talk. Your imagination then works on ways to present your ideas creatively. Collation of the relevant material comes next, which is then transposed onto paper, and finally delivered as a speech.

EXERCISE 21
STORYTELLING FROM PICTURES

Nowadays there are many beautiful greetings cards on the market. Collect a few of these for this exercise. Choose those that appeal to you and are interesting in content, such as reproductions of paintings, preferably with people in them.

Choose a quiet moment, relax in a chair, and study one of these cards. Look at the colour and texture, the shapes and contents of the card. Now describe what you see.

When you have studied the card, become more involved with the subject matter. Imagine stepping into the picture. For example, the card might depict a family sitting or playing on the beach. Envisage yourself as a member of that family, a guest, or passer-by. Establish what your relationship is within that group, and observe what might be going on around you. Speak your thoughts.

As you become more confident with this exercise, you can use a tape-recorder to monitor your use of language and vocabulary. Play the tape back and assess yourself for fluency and accuracy.

EXERCISE 22
READING AND RETELLING A STORY

To encourage memory, accuracy and concentration, read aloud a short fable or fairy story. Then retell it, using your own words.

EXERCISE 23
READING ON TAPE

You may prefer to read your text when giving a speech, rather than using prompt cards (see page 83). If so, check your ability to sight-read by taping yourself reading aloud. If on playback you think it lacks flow and is verbally inaccurate, then your sight-reading is weak and would benefit from practice.

For business presentations, precision can be essential. Read aloud a little every day and you will improve.

Remember to mark where you are going to take your breath pauses. This will help your flow.

Aim to glance ahead when you are reading, so that your peripheral vision is aware of the text before you speak it.

When checking your recorded passage against your written text, underline words that have been mispronounced or left out, and then repeat the same exercise until you get it right.

Underline words that you find hard to pronounce. Rehearse these repeatedly until you feel comfortable saying them.

speechmakers' bible

chapter 2

Preparing
and planning

We have all been on the receiving end of a poorly planned speech or presentation; perhaps it was pitched at the wrong level, seemed to have no direction and structure or went on for too long. Giving effective speeches should be like a master sportsman playing at the highest level – we may only see a sublime performance of an hour or so before the spectators and cameras, but before the game, weeks, months and years of training and preparation have been invested unseen to deliver the result on the day. In the same way, people often remark 'he's a natural' or 'she just got up and looked so in control...she's a natural'. What the audience doesn't realize is that these 'naturals' have often spent hours in planning and preparation behind the scenes to ensure that they deliver the result.

Planning your speech

What is involved in planning and preparing? One of the most important rules, and one ignored by a great many people, is to prepare well in advance.

Start by considering who the audience is and what your goal is. Ask yourself why you've been asked to speak. Are you the father of the bride? Perhaps you are an expert on local history? Is it because you are an extrovert and known for being humorous? Or is this a business presentation to be made to gain new business or inform your staff? This will allow you to gather relevant and compelling material, including stories and quotes. This material then needs to be structured in such a way that it helps the audience to follow the flow and keep you on track. If applicable, you will need to consider what visual aids will assist in reaching your objective (see page 67). At this stage, you can then move on to rehearsals, which will provide the final polish. By thorough preparation you will ensure that when you take to the stage you will be at the top of your game.

Length

Probably the most common error when giving a speech or presentation is going on for too long. Unless we are faced with an outstanding speaker, few are the times when we've remarked: 'I wish that speech had gone on and on.' When we are in the audience we are quick to point out the fact that the speaker has gone well over their allotted time; however, when we get up to speak we often trip into the very same trap. Why is this?

As we sit down and write speeches and presentations we look at a few pages of notes or a 30-page Powerpoint presentation and think to ourselves: 'We'll be through that in no time.' But when we start talking we find out differently, people arrive late, so we don't start on time, questions are asked, we go off script and digress. Before we know it our time is up and we're only halfway through.

Conversely, however, if your speech is too short it may seem rude and people may feel short-changed`.

So, how do we get the timing right?

Most importantly, rehearse out loud – reading it in your head just won't do. A dress rehearsal will allow you to fine-tune your timings. Ideally you should practise with a live audience member who can act and react as if it was the real thing, asking a number of questions that you can brainstorm between you.

If appropriate, plan time for questions – 25% is not unreasonable, so if you have an hour slot you'll actually just be making a 45-minute presentation.

Give yourself some contingency time. This will enable you to cope easily with a late start or audience reaction.

If you're using Powerpoint, a very rough guide is to allow three to five minutes per slide. It's a chilling thought that ten slides could therefore sometimes support a one-hour presentation! However, this is approximate and should never replace live rehearsal.

Consider your audience

Understanding your audience is the key step to making your speech tailored and relevant. Imagine you were selling a mobile phone to your grandmother: you might stress the security aspects, large buttons and volume control. However, if you were describing the same phone to a teenager, you would make a completely different presentation on its colour, texting capabilities and built-in camera. In the same way you need to adapt your speech to your audience.

Here is a checklist of information that you should ask yourself:

- How many people?
- What are their ages?
- What is the gender mix?
- What ideas, feelings or experiences do you have in common?
- Do they have strong religious beliefs?
- How would they view humour?
- What would they like to hear in the speech?
- Are there words or topics better left unsaid?
- What language do they use?
- Are there local customs or prejudices to be aware of?
- What is their culture?
- What is their style?
- What is their level of knowledge of your subject?
- What is motivating them?
- What presentation style will work best for them?
- Will they need visual aids?
- Will they need to hear a lot of data, facts and statistics?
- What is their work background, social background, education level?
- What are they especially proud of or loyal to?
- Whose opinion do they respect?
- Have you accommodated the politics or relationship tensions that are involved in the presentation situation?

Of course, the best way to answer these questions is to speak beforehand to as many members of the audience as possible. You probably won't be able to account for all of these elements, so the key considerations are to ascertain the predominant style of the audience and what *not* to say in order to avoid offence.

Cultural barriers

Cultural differences are evident in nearly every aspect of day-to-day life, and presentations and speeches are no different. When you are speaking in your native tongue that is not that of the audience you need to make allowances. You should make extra preparation, adapt the delivery of your speech, ensure the content is plain and simple and, if appropriate, use supporting visual aids to improve comprehension.

Preparation

Habits and behaviour in different cultures are continually evolving and changing and so what may have been true in the past doesn't necessarily hold for the present. The modern and sensible method, as with any audience, is to obtain information on the correct approach by speaking to them beforehand. Get a member of the foreign audience and ask them to listen to a full rehearsal and give you feedback on your delivery style, visual aids and content. You'll then get more accurate and relevant advice on the effectiveness of your communication. Specifically, you may request comments on:

- energy levels
- eye contact
- standing or sitting
- words and expressions used
- dress
- questions and answers
- nonverbal communication and body language

Delivery skills

The populations of the English-speaking countries are not renowned for their linguistic capabilities. Sometimes we forget or are ignorant of just how challenging it is to operate in another language, be it speaking or listening. To aid understanding, speakers should use pausing and pace. By pausing, the speaker allows the audience a short time to translate and digest what has just been said. An unfortunate side effect for many of the tension they experience when speaking in public is that they speed up. This is the opposite of what non-English speaking audiences require. Speakers should slow the pace to facilitate understanding and to avoid running words into each other.

Content

The key to content with non-native English speaking audiences is to keep it plain and simple:

- Where a simple word exists, use it! For example, say 'now' rather than 'at the present juncture'.
- Avoid idioms, abbreviations and acronyms.
- Exercise extreme caution with humour.
- Keep it short. Listening in another language takes some concentration and we all have limited attention spans.
- Learn a few phrases in the language of the audience and use them to top and tail the speech, it will help build connection.
- Never criticize the local country, even in jest.

Visual aids (see also page 67)

Visual aids take on a special and subtly different significance with non-English speaking audiences. If the audience 'miss' the occasional word they can refer to a slide or other visual aid to pick up the word or gain context, which will assist them in making an educated guess as to its meaning. This may be one of the occasional instances where reading from a slide may be acceptable.

Equally, handouts can allow people to read through the content of the speech where they don't catch the speaker's words, or to study the detail in their own time.

See Chapter Six for more help on using visual aids.

Obtaining material

It is an often recited fact that how someone communicates makes a much greater impression on people than what they actually say.

However, the impression created does not necessarily equate to how effective the speech is and trying to ad-lib with an unprepared speech is a dangerous road to go down, leading as it might to accusations of style over substance. Therefore, it is important to have accurate, relevant and interesting reference material. This material comes from two places: what you know and from research you carry out.

What you know

It is likely that if you are giving the speech you will have a wealth of experience and knowledge to be used as reference material. As we have noted, in order to refine the material it is helpful to ask yourself two questions: who is the audience and what is the objective of the presentation? By doing this you'll be able to review the mass of potential content and turn it into pertinent data. For example, if a great scientist is addressing schoolchildren to introduce them to electricity, he or she will choose just a limited, relevant and interesting part of their overall knowledge.

Researched material

Reference material can be divided into the following categories:

Facts: Make sure they are facts. Just because you've picked up a piece of information on the Internet doesn't make it a fact. Try and check it out from at least two supporting places.

Statistics: Always be clear on the exact basis of the statistics – for example, what population, what period. There are few things more embarrassing than being caught out not knowing your source.

Quotes and testimonials: These are frequently employed for formal occasions such as speeches.

Stories and case studies: Useful for illustrating and proving points, as well as beginning your speech.

Personal anecdotes: People's own experiences are often far more interesting and engagingly related than forced regurgitation of other people's humour.

Jokes and humorous stories: As ever with humour, be careful: is it appropriate to the audience, is it too old or just not funny?

You'll find a good source of useful reference material in Chapter Eight.

Sources

Asking people: Researched material is rarely completely up to date or applicable to the audience. Why not speak to some of the audience in advance or, if it's a business presentation, do some 'mystery shopping' by pretending to be a customer.

Books: As with any source of information, it is always worthwhile cross-referencing your facts to make sure they are accurate. As with the Internet, just because it's in print doesn't make it true.

Libraries: Not only a free and extensive supply of books, libraries now have a wealth of other information, be it local information, microfiche, the Internet and, perhaps most importantly, librarians to guide you quickly through the maze.

Internet: The Internet is a phenomenal galaxy of information to support speechmakers and presenters, but its greatest strength is at times its biggest pitfall – the sheer amount of information out there can make it difficult to find exactly what you need. When using a search engine try and use advanced search terms such as inverted commas to find exact matches.

Additionally, get a large sheet of paper and note down everything you can think of that will be relevant to your speech. As you go about your daily work, write down on paper any ideas that spring to mind and file them away. Apart from saving yourself work later on, having some initial material provides a comforting buffer when you come to start writing.

Thinking before writing

Before you start to write, here are some points to consider:

• Know exactly what your subject is and how far you are going to take it. (More specific guidance for business presentations, after-dinner speaking, weddings and other celebrations is given in the relevant chapters.)

• Ask yourself: 'What do the audience really want to know?'

• Will the important facts be highlighted?

• Will the talk be clear and easy to understand?

• Is there a strong theme throughout? (Avoid too much padding or deviation from the point.)

- Will there be a time limit (see above)? Check that you will be able to keep to it.

- Will it be possible to introduce pictorial language? Is it too abstract?

- Will the speech be presented in such a way that listeners will find it easy to retain?

- Is there too much information?

- Will you use visual aids? Where will they fit in? Will the venue be set up for them? (See page 67 for advice on using visual aids.)

Remember to:

- Use simple and direct language wherever possible.

- Be grammatically correct and clear in delivery.

- Adopt a bright and cheerful style, without being trite or trivial.

It's important to speak the language your audience will understand. If you are to make a speech to an audience who know relatively little about your subject, using highly technical jargon will fog the listeners and lose their interest. But pepper your talk with personal experiences and stories and you will highlight your message and illustrate the technical points in a simple and uncomplicated way. On the other hand, you may be talking to a professional group of colleagues, in which case more detailed technicalities will not be out of place, although you should be warned off overloading the listeners with too much data. The brain can absorb only so much at any one time.

Talking in pictures will improve the ambience. Look for places where you can lighten with pictorial colour. If you dislike telling a joke for fear of it falling flat (see Chapter Eight for more advice about this), tell a story instead. It will add charm and zest to your speech.

 EXERCISE 24
DEVELOPING YOUR POWERS OF IMAGERY

Read the phrases below and open your mind to the various images they suggest. Picture them as you read aloud the following:

- bright buttoned stars
- melting moments
- vibrating motorways
- steep steps
- wold-wooded Worcestershire
- fast and slick
- momentous moment
- monotonous monologue
- energetic exercises
- chocolate truffles
- massive machinery
- thrilling races

Figures of speech that can be used for impact

Metaphors and similes

These can stimulate audience imagination, and add speech impact. Use them sparingly and with discretion for maximum impact.

Avoid mixing metaphors, such as in the following: 'Gentlemen, the seed of disharmony has been sown among us. If it is not nipped in the bud, it will burst into a huge blaze that will flood the whole planet.'

Rhetorical questions

The speaker asks a question that does not demand a reply. This intensifies dramatic impact and involves the speaker more closely with the audience. For example:

- 'Why are we here today? We are here to address the problem of litter in our community.'

- 'What are the main principles of a marriage?'

The inflection of your voice should not rise on the question, but end on a downward note. The former method demands an answer, whereas the latter does not.

Antithesis

Focus on contrasts to set one idea against another. For example:

- 'You played with him; I worked with him.'

- 'You taught; I was your student.'

- 'You go; we stay.'

Repetition

By using this, points of issue can be reinforced. For example:

- 'We will win. We will win, not lose.'

- 'Pause awhile and think; think what this will mean.'

Words and phrases to avoid

Avoid using terms such as:

- 'on this *auspicious* occasion'

- 'this most *prestigious* building'

- '*would like to say a few words*' (when you mean *'make a speech'* or *'give a talk on'*)

- 'my *grateful* thanks'

- 'very pleased' (*pleased* is sufficient)

- 'those ones' (*those* and *ones* mean the same)

- 'sole monopoly' (*sole* and *monopoly* mean the same)

- 'actually', 'frankly', 'as a matter of fact' (all superfluous words)

Clichés and superfluous expressions

Try to avoid these. Some examples are:

- sort of
- you know
- I mean
- in this day and age
- basically speaking
- tell me about it
- by and large
- be that as it may
- the fact of the matter is
- at the end of the day
- let's face it
- all things considered
- to be honest
- fair enough
- same difference
- just one of those things

The other danger with clichés, particularly at weddings and celebrations, when you might be tempted to say: 'May all their troubles be little ones', is that older members of the audience may have heard them before and indeed the previous speaker may use the same joke or saying.

The plan of your speech

The following guidelines will help you plan a speech for a social occasion, such as a meeting of a club or society, when your approach to your audience needs to be friendly and informal. However, the formats for social and business presentations are generally similar, with a few possible variations:

- Introductions may be minimal in content, stating briefly but clearly and with vitality the areas that are to be covered and how they will be broached. This may apply more readily to presentations given within a company and among colleagues.

- A business presentation may need to contain more compacted information, with the additional back-up of visual aids and handouts.

- There can be a greater need for precision and more sharply focused material, with occasional summaries to ensure clarity.

- There may be more statements of facts – for example, statistics and data information.

For guidance on business presentations, see Chapter Six.

Structure

Like most human endeavours, a speech needs a beginning, a middle and an ending. In the introduction, you are establishing contact with the audience and indicating the theme of your talk; in the middle you are giving the main information; in the ending you are drawing the threads together and reiterating the most important points. In other words, as someone once said: 'First I tell 'em what I'm going to tell 'em. Then I tell 'em. Then I tell 'em what I've told them.'

Introduction

Introductions should be attractive. They don't need to be startlingly dramatic, but they should aim at being imaginative. That way the audience will want more.

So how do you create a good first impression and start off on the right foot with the introduction? One way, if appropriate, is to talk to the listeners in a conversational and warm manner, and to imagine that you are speaking to a close friend who is sitting at the back of the hall.

Typically, there are three parts to the introduction:

• opening comments
• engagement item and link
• subject and agenda

Opening comments

The aim of the opening comments is to remove distractions from the audience's mind. As they enter the room or are waiting for your speech, they will be thinking of a whole range of things, a lot of them not related to what you are about to say: 'Have I paid the bills?', 'How long is this going to last?', 'I wonder if my house sale has gone through?', 'Am I going to get a cigarette break?' To ensure that these thoughts are banished so that the audience is free to concentrate on what is about to be said, the effective speechmaker needs to use well-crafted opening comments of introduction and 'housekeeping'. Here are some examples of typical areas covered in the opening comments:

- Welcome and greeting.
- Introducing and naming yourself and any other speakers.
- Telling the audience how long you will be speaking for.
- Indicating whether you'll be stopping for any breaks.
- Inviting questions as you go or asking for them to be kept until the end.
- Letting the audience know where relevant facilities such as toilets and fire escapes, etc. are located.
- Asking them to switch off mobile phones and other electronic devices that might distract.
- Letting them know whether they'll need to take notes or if there will be a handout of the content and any visual aids used.
- If it is a more formal presentation, letting them know what the specific objective of the talk is and what, if anything, you won't be covering.

EXAMPLE OF OPENING COMMENTS:

'Good morning and welcome. I'm Jack Griffiths, head of the Parent–teacher Association and I'm going to be talking to you for the next 45 minutes about the plan for developing the school's extracurricular activities for our pupils.

I want this to be as interactive as possible so please ask me questions whenever they arise. If you haven't been to the school before, the toilets are just opposite the door where you came in and in the unlikely event of a fire we'll leave through the doors behind me and assemble in the main car park.

I'd be most grateful if you could switch off your mobile phones for the duration of the talk so we have minimum interruptions as I know some of you need to be away promptly at 7 o'clock. So if there are no further points let's crack straight on.'

Engagement item and link

Having removed any distractions with opening comments, you may then choose to use an engagement item and link.

The purpose of an engagement item (if used) is to grab the attention of the audience. Typically, when mentioned, people immediately think of a joke. The engagement item can be a joke, but as we have seen earlier, jokes represent a high-risk approach at one of the most critical times of the speech.

Fortunately, engagement items are not limited to jokes. They can be anything used to attract the interest of listeners and leave them wanting to hear more. When planning your speech, here are a few ideas of different sources for an engagement item:

- **An anecdote:** An anecdote often draws a more natural and conversational style from the speaker as opposed to a more formal style that may be created by the tension present at the start of the speech. [See also Chapter Eight.]

- **A personal story:** Personal stories have the advantage that they don't need learning and are much more easily related with real emotion and feeling. It can be something as simple as recounting an incident that happened during the speaker's journey to the venue.

- **A clip of video:** Video and film have the advantage of often having been created with the goal of entertaining and can rapidly transfix audiences and put an end to their chatter. Companies often use 'talking heads' of customers discussing their products or service.

- **A photograph, prop or other visual aid:** What we see is often a lot more powerful than what we hear. By showing a powerful image we can short-cut the time it takes to engage people. At a speech it could be an unusual photo of the subject of the speech, perhaps as a baby.

- **A quote or saying:** A favourite of speechmakers, relevant quotes are often easy to find using the Internet and reference books. Care has to be taken that the quote chosen is not too clichéd. A collection of quotes related to a number of different subject areas is included in Chapter Eight.

- **A stunt:** Be it riding in on a Harley Davidson or swinging on a trapeze, stunts can be a dynamic way of making sure people are switched on to what's coming next.

- **A common thread between you and the audience:** This could be what you have in common with the audience, a time when you were in the same audience or the last time you were speaking with them. All serve to create a connection between you and them.

- **Provocation:** Stirring up emotions is certainly a good way of getting their attention. However, be careful you don't go over the top. A typical way could be to kick off by expressing an opinion completely at odds with current accepted thinking or the audience's point of view.

Engagement items should, wherever possible and especially with business presentations, be relevant to the subject of the talk, rather than some random witticism recently heard by the speechmaker.

If an engagement item is used it must then be connected and made relevant to your chosen topic by using a link such as: '...which leads me to today's subject...' Having named the subject, the speaker is then in a position to 'tell 'em what they're going to tell 'em' with the agenda.

The agenda

The agenda simply tells the audience what they are about to hear. In less business-related environments there is no need for the speaker to use the rather formal word 'agenda'. A simpler way is to tell the audience what you're going to cover. For example: 'Today I'm going to talk about fruit. First, I'll talk about apples, then I'm going to talk about oranges and, finally, I'm going to discuss bananas.'

The body of the speech

The main facts and/or arguments go into this section.

Some people find it easier to write the body of the speech first, followed by the conclusion. They then insert the introduction last of all. For the first draft this may be the easier way. It is a matter of choice.

Know how long the speech will run. If time is short, the talk should be balanced in such a way that the audience is not overloaded with too many details. A longer speech, however, may handle more information.

Make the most forceful point last. This gives weight to the speech and will assist delivery when building the talk to a climax.

If a speech is well structured in content (like a well-written poem), it will trace itself through the various nuances, guiding the speaker to perform at his or her best.

How to include statistics

Just because you say so doesn't make it so. Picture a snake oil salesman or a carpetbagger (or even a politician, come to think of it); they make many assertions during speeches, but why should we believe them? One of the key forms of content when giving a speech is statistics, but how to use them to their maximum effect?

Reliable sourcing: As with any form of reference material, it's vital that the source is rock-solid reliable. Few things are more embarrassing to a speaker than to have the whole performance undermined by the unearthing of a poor or incorrect statistic in the mix. If using visual aids mark the source clearly on the aid.

Clarity of data: On a similar theme, be honest about sample sizes, time periods and extent of the data. If it comes out when you are centre stage that you've been economical with the truth or shown only a tiny fraction of the data that supports your case your credibility will be destroyed.

Use visual aids (see page 67): Visual aids bring statistics to life. A string of numbers means very little, but when translated into a graph the effect is transformed. The speaker should examine the statistics and choose between types of chart such as line, bar and pie to select the format that will have the most impact on the audience.

Analogies: If the statistic consists of single numbers, visual aids may not be the most appropriate way of bringing them to life. An analogy or image may help drive the point home.

Saying Bill Gates will soon become a trillionaire means little to normal people, but the scale of his wealth is perhaps better illustrated by the following example from the *Daily Telegraph* of using an analogy to put things into understandable terms:

> *The stage is now set for Mr Gates to become the world's first trillionaire.*

> *The* Daily Telegraph *reports that having made about $4,566,000 for every hour of the past year, and with his wealth growing at the 61% compound annual rate it has enjoyed so far, he will hit the $1,000,000,000,000 mark in 2004.*

> *The paper also states that his current wealth exceeds the economic output of all but the 18 wealthiest nations.*

> *In fact, if his wealth continues to snowball, his fortune will overtake Britain's gross national product in 2005.*

How to bring in stories/quotes

One of the greatest challenges faced by presenters is the phenomenon that frequently occurs when they feel under the tension of being observed by an audience: they stop being themselves. One way in which this manifests itself is that speakers start using over-formal language and become over-reliant on a boring stream of facts, lists, statements and information.

A simple way to break out of this cycle is by the use of storytelling, since audiences often want to see a more human and engaging presenter displaying some of his or her personality. Bland statements on their own are often less easy to understand or relate to compared with a story that illustrates the real meaning. Stories are also often used as the engagement item during the opening of a speech or presentation to get the attention of the audience. Stories should be relevant to the content of the speech and may either be related directly to the subject matter or could be an allegory. Stories can often take the form of 'before, event, after', where the story revolves around how the event or the stimulus changed the situation between the before and after.

PERSONAL STORY: COMPARE THE STATEMENT: 'WIMBLEDON IS A WORLD-CLASS SPORTING EVENT' WITH:

'As I grew up, my Mother was always glued to the Wimbledon fortnight on the television, but for me it just didn't hold any excitement, but that all changed when I actually went. When I emerged as a spectator into the arena on a blistering summer's day, the atmosphere took my breath away – the colours, the movement of the players and the sheer electricity created by the crowd; I'll never forget it.'

ALLEGORY: COMPARE A STATEMENT: 'PREPARATION AND REHEARSAL FOR SPEECHMAKING IS VITAL' WITH:

'Good speechmaking is like playing golf. Top players do not sit around all year waiting for tournaments. They practise day in day out, attempting to perfect every tiny aspect of their game. As a percentage of their overall training time, match time represents a minute amount. In the same way, many of the 'naturals' have often spent many hours putting in the preparation and rehearsal time for a peak performance on the day.'

Storytelling should not be done just for the sake of it. Either the story should be directly relevant to the overall speech or presentation, or it should be made relevant by drawing the link between the story you have just told. [See also Chapter Eight.]

Building to a climax

The climax is the site of greatest interest, achieved via the arrangement of points addressed in ascending order, and culminating in an plethora of ideas.

When you come to deliver the speech, the thoughts should precede the words. It is the increased intensity of thought, allied with necessary modulations of pitch, pause, power, emphasis and pace, that lead to the climax.

EXERCISE 25
BUILDING TO A CLIMAX

Practise the following. Use thought to guide your voice, emphasis to underline meaning, and increased pace, power and intensity in accordance with the action.

John climbed the chestnut tree.
Higher and higher he went
Until he reached the very top.

Alec struck the firework into the earth. The paper smouldered, the powder ignited, there was a build-up of pressure and the hot gases were expelled rearwards. With a burst of light, the rocket was launched – WHOOSH!

If we are to succeed,
If we are to win the race against time,
We must act now,
And we must act fast!

The ending

It's an old saying that people remember two parts of speeches – the beginning and the end. The end will be fresh in the minds of the audience as they leave and can be vital to retention of your messages. There are three parts to the end of speeches and presentations: the summary, the conclusion and, if appropriate, the question and answer session. Speechmakers often mix the first two or just don't know the difference.

The summary

Summaries are optional. For non-businesses speeches they may destroy the tone: summarizing a wedding speech just wouldn't make sense. They are more appropriate to business presentations. A summary is a recapitulation of the points that have been made in the body of the speech, and its purpose is firstly to help the audience to retain the key ideas. Secondly, there will always be moments when the attention of the listeners will wander. By summarizing, the speaker has a second chance to plug this gap. In a true summary there is no new information covered.

The conclusion

A conclusion is different. The conclusion is the 'so now what' of the speech and can take various forms, such as:

- **Next steps/actions:** The things that need doing are assigned to different parties with a date and time for their completion.

- **A recommendation:** If the pros and cons of a number of different options have been presented, this may lead logically to a recommendation based on these factors.

- **A call to action:** This may be a request for help, a donation or a change of direction. At a wedding or formal occasion, it may be where the speaker calls upon the audience to rise and make a toast.

- **A request for a decision:** In the case of a presentation to persuade, the main body of the speech may have been the case to convince the audience and the reasons why.

EXAMPLE OF SUMMARY AND CONCLUSION FOR A PRESENTATION WITHOUT A QUESTION AND ANSWER SESSION

'So let's review our three options for travelling to the upcoming event in Paris.

Firstly, we looked at driving to Dover, taking the ferry to Calais and then driving on to the French capital. The principal advantage will be having our car with us when we get there; however, that comes at a considerable cost, both in terms of time and money.

Secondly, we discussed taking the Eurostar. This choice would take us directly to the centre of Paris in an impressively quick time at a special winter rate. Unfortunately that would mean we'd have to travel from our office in the outskirts of London in to Waterloo Station by cab, which would add to the cost.

Finally, there was the option of flying. As we are located in west London, this would give us a relatively short trip to Heathrow followed by a very quick flight. The drawback would be the length of time it then takes to get to central Paris from the airport, which would be significant.

In conclusion, therefore, I'm recommending we take the Eurostar. To get things moving I'd like Paul to book tickets by Friday and Jane to reserve the taxis by next Tuesday.'

Planning and preparing for questions

Question and answer sessions are often poorly planned. Even when time has been spent preparing the body of the presentation, speakers often neglect to prepare for what they may be asked. Areas to consider when preparing for questions include:

- Who is the audience?

- What are their issues?

- What are they likely to ask?

- Who is best placed to brainstorm potential questions?

- What examples and visual aids will help answer their questions?

- If you are one of several speakers will one of you act as chairperson?

- Who is going to lead answers on each topic?

- Are there any questions you won't answer due to their sensitivity?

- How will you deal with questions that you don't know the answer to?

- How will you deal with questions when you know the answer to them will be coming up later in the speech?

As with the main body of the presentation, the question and answer session should also be rehearsed. To accomplish this, the speaker or speakers should firstly write down all the potential questions they may be asked and prepare their answers. An independent person should then be armed with these questions and rehearse the speaker or speakers in how to respond to them. At the same time, the mock audience member should throw in new questions to ensure the speaker is accustomed to thinking on the spot.

This section examined planning for questions at the end of the speech/presentation; later, in Chapter Six, we will look at how to handle questions during the speech or presentation. The three deadly sins of ending a speech must be avoided at all costs:

- **Not having an ending:** We have all probably been at a speech or presentation that has just stopped dead or flipped straight to 'any questions?' without warning. This leaves audiences with the impression that you couldn't wait to finish.

- **Overrunning:** This is normally the product of lack of planning and rehearsal. Listeners are likely to switch off unless you are highly entertaining and interesting or they have a compelling reason to listen.

- **'Just one more thing...':** Adding extra points or those you have forgotten indicates lack of control and detracts from the coherence of your message. They are also likely to be delivered with insufficient conviction.

Visual aids

'A picture paints a thousand words.' One of the key ways that a speech differs from a presentation is that the former rarely has visual aids. They have become synonymous with presentations, particularly in a business context. When used appropriately they can add dramatically to the effectiveness of a presentation.

Among some of the purposes they are useful for are:

• Illustrating a point being made by the speaker.

• Bringing a series of numbers or set of data to life in a graph or chart.

• Variety.

• Adding interest by providing the audience with a different visual stimulus other than just watching the speaker.

• Serving as a prompt to the speaker of the upcoming content.

• Reinforcing what the speaker is saying.

• Assisting non-native language speakers with comprehension.

However, as speakers have come to depend more and more upon visual aids, in many cases they have become over-reliant upon them, complacent, or their use has become riddled with errors, as we shall examine later. When used correctly, they should be a support to the speaker, rather than the other way round with the visual aids taking over. This has become so much the case that the word 'presentation' has gone from meaning the whole event to also meaning the set of visuals such as a Powerpoint slide show.

Choosing the type of visual aid

A common default now is to immediately reach for Powerpoint when considering which type of visual aids to use. But Powerpoint is just one of the available media to support presentations. To decide which will be most suitable, speakers should take into account the following considerations:

- The number of people in the audience.

- The size of the presenting space.

- The style of the audience.

- The degree of formality of the occasion.

- The complexity of the content.

- Whether the visuals will need to be altered during the presentation.

TYPES OF VISUAL AID

None! A good question speakers should always ask themselves is: 'Do I really need visual aids? Will using visual aids help me or hinder me in achieving my aims?'

Powerpoint projection: Powerpoint is useful for presentations with larger audiences where the speaker needs to control the pace. However, it can reduce the amount of focus on the speaker, appear overly formal, or trip up the less technically aware.

Handouts or 'pitchbooks': These create a less formal environment and are good for small gatherings. The audience can record their thoughts on the handouts and take them away. The disadvantage is that the speaker has no control over which page the audience is looking at – overeager people will always turn straight to the last page.

Laptop computer screen: When speaking to small groups of two or three people the speaker may use his or her laptop screen. It means they can maintain control and the informality of a seated environment. As always with electronic support, danger lies in using Powerpoint if not completely comfortable with it. When presenting from a laptop, back-up is essential.

Flipcharts: When presenting in informal settings with smaller groups, flipcharts are often a suitable support. They are particularly useful when there are high degrees of interaction and feedback being captured from the audience, such as when 'facilitating'. Due to their size and positioning, they are unsuitable for larger audiences. In some environments they may also not create the necessary levels of 'professionalism'.

Overhead projector (OHP) images: OHPs are fast becoming out of date. They require considerable preparation and care to ensure a good image, but can still prove a useful support for larger audiences. The frames of the acetates are particularly useful for writing notes on. However, they take some time to prepare and bulbs have a knack of blowing at the wrong moment.

DVD/Video: These are useful as an engagement item at the beginning of a presentation, and will also give the speaker a moment to gather his or her thoughts. Speakers must be familiar with the operation of the DVD player or video so that it will commence immediately on cue and to avoid any embarrassing silences and frantic manipulation of remote controls.

Pictures/Posters: When the speaker needs to refer to certain images throughout the presentation they may position pictures around the room. This is also useful if the speaker needs to link a number of different visual aids or to tell a story through them.

Physical objects: With smaller audiences, handing items round involves a high degree of engagement. However, this can be a distraction and is normally best avoided unless highly controlled.

Creating visual aids

A common error when preparing for a new presentation is to start with visual aids. This should come only after considering your audience, goal and how you will structure the content.

When these steps have been carried out, and you have decided to use visual aids of a specific type, you are ready to create them. There are no absolute rules for creating visual aids, but certain guidelines are useful:

- **Have a title:** Titles help guide your audience and should summarize the content.

- **The rule of two:** Where possible, try to keep paragraphs to a maximum of two lines. Audiences get rapidly turned off by huge amounts of text on visuals. Another side effect of having large amounts of text in complete sentences is that audiences tend to read them – and when they start reading they stop listening to you. Conversely, if you use single words there is a danger that they will not serve as a sufficient prompt to remind you what you were going to say, nor does it assist your audience in understanding the point you are making.

- **Colours:** Colours add variety to visual aids provided they do not degrade the readability of the visual. This happens frequently with dark-coloured backgrounds, when it is vital to use a white or very near-white font. If employing a normal white background avoid light fonts. This is particularly relevant when colours are projected because they may change; what appears clear on your laptop isn't necessarily going to come out equally as clearly on a screen.

- **Create your notes when you create your visual aids:** A useful form of notes can be the storyboard, where you print out an abridged version of your visuals, perhaps six to a page. Numbering these will help you move from section to section.

- **Use a large enough font size:** Check that the visuals are readable from the back of the room.

- **Use charts/graphs:** If you need to show a series of numbers and figures, use a suitable chart or graph.

- **Use images/pictures:** Consider using images and pictures for more expressive or dynamic audiences. However, don't use them for the sake of it. They should be relevant, original and of good-quality reproduction.

Interacting with visual aids

When speakers use visual aids, they often spend too much time looking at them and not at the audience. This is caused by a combination of the tension the speaker feels combined with the fact that most of the audience are looking at the visual aid – which also draws the speaker to it. It is not unusual to see a speaker glance at just one visual 20–30 times!

To avoid this, you should maintain eye contact with the audience when using visual aids. A good technique is known as 'load, aim, fire'. You 'load' the idea in your mind and turn to the audience, 'aiming' at a particular person or section of larger audiences, without speaking. You then 'fire', or continue talking.

TIPS FOR USING VISUAL AIDS

Always have back-up: It sometimes feels like electronic support devices have been designed to go wrong at the most inconvenient times. Speakers should always have back-up such as a spare laptop, handouts, or a copy of the presentation on a disk or 'memory stick'.

Make good transitions between visuals: Too often, speakers put up their next visual and appear surprised by it, undermining their credibility. A good speaker introduces and positions the visual before showing it, leaving an impression of preparedness and competence.

Prepare and practice with the equipment you are going to use: Practice is vital in terms of becoming familiar not only with the visuals, but also how the equipment works. How do the lights work? How does your laptop connect to the projector? Are there any flip chart pens? Is there a power extension lead? Will their laptop be able to run the software you have used?

Have someone else read through your visual aids for errors: Of course it is important that you read through your visual aids, both to spot errors and to familiarize yourself with them. The danger is that we often read what we want to read and miss blatant gaffes such as 'the the' in a sentence that isn't highlighted by a 'spell check.'

Finally, less is more: By this we mean fewer visuals with fewer words will very often have more impact.

Common errors with visual aids:

- **Too many visuals:** This is probably the most common error and usually comes from speakers who feel they need everything on their slides in case they forget. This is frequently referred to as 'Death by Powerpoint'. A way of avoiding this is to imagine each slide taking three to five minutes to talk through. This indicates that 10 slides may be enough for an hour-long presentation with a question and answer session.

- **Too much information on a visual:** The speaker usually produces the visual and announces: 'This is a busy slide' or 'You won't be able to read this but...' 'But I couldn't be bothered to make a suitable visual' is what they mean. Speakers should restrict themselves to one key concept per visual.

- **Curse of clip-art:** When Powerpoint arrived as a support to presenting, using clip-art pictures pasted into slides was new to audiences. Those days are gone, the images all too familiar and it smacks of desperation when the speaker inserts the picture of a stick man scratching his head under a question mark. See the guidelines above for ideas for good images.

- **Too many builds and effects:** To make their presentation more interesting, speakers sometimes feel obliged to use effects. Builds, where one line or item appears at a time, can focus attention, but if too many points are built the speaker ends up going continually back to their laptop to bring in the next one. Effects, where the next slide flies in or rolls in, top to bottom, etc., should be simple and consistent. In 99% of cases sound effects should be reserved for children's presentations.

SUMMARY CHECKLIST: PREPARING AND PLANNING

How long do you need to speak for?

What are the demographics of your audience – do you have to take any cultural differences into account?

Have you planned any reference material (facts/ statistics/stories/anecdotes) carefully – is it relevant, accurate and interesting?

Are there any metaphors or similes that you could use to help get your message across in a way that will make it easier to understand without using clichés?

Have you remembered the basic structure:
- Introduction (opening comments/engagement item/ link/subject and agenda)
- Body (this is where any statstics, visual aids, stories or quotes will go)
- Climax (it's not what you say but how you say it)
- Ending (summary/conclusion)

Do you know how any question and answer session will be organised and how will you handle difficult questions?

Have you chosen the right medium for any visual aids? Are they clear, relevant and accurate and do you know how any electrical equipment works?

speechmakers' bible

chapter 3

Writing
your speech

Now you are ready to start writing your speech. You need to have a genuine interest in the topic on which you are to speak. Make it your own from the beginning. This can help stimulate the brain and get it moving. Your thoughts, your ideas help to create a personal touch that can in turn generate enthusiasm, a positive anticipation and a wish to do well. If a talk is based purely on the accumulation of knowledge acquired solely from books, your speech may lack pizzazz and personal magnetism. Begin by jotting down your own ideas and build from there.

The first draft

Choose a time of day when you can work without interruption. Sit down and start writing, using any collated material that appeals and which you think is relevant. If a fact or an idea reminds you of a story, write it down. At this early stage you can allow your mind the freedom of expression. Whether or not you use all the material written at this time is not so important. The crucial factor is to get started and to create. The imagination may be inhibited if too many boundaries are introduced too early.

Develop the habit of writing in the way in which you speak, because it is you that your audience wants to hear. It may also help your ideas to flow more easily.

The second draft

This is the stage at which you groom your speech. Before you begin, reread your first draft and then ask yourself:

- How do I view myself?

- Who are my audience?

- How do I view them?

- How would I like them to view me?

- What will my audience gain from my speech?

- What do I hope to gain from my speech?

These points will help you to link with your audience before you've even seen them. Keep them at the back of your mind as you prepare your second draft.

You may at this stage of development need to rewrite your existing material. However, with the main ideas set down on paper in the first draft, this should not be a daunting task. Determine an outline. You might ask yourself: 'What is my theme? How far do I want to take it?' Keep within the parameters that you set yourself. In the original draft you tapped your creative skills by permitting yourself to think broadly about your subject. Now you can afford to discipline your work and thus build a format, without being in danger of losing the heart of your speech and the spontaneity of your ideas.

As already stated in Chapter Two, a speech needs a beginning, a middle and an end. Because you have written the first draft, most of your material and the substance of your speech are probably all there, and just need to be moulded into shape. If you decide to work on the middle of your talk first, remember that ideas or arguments need to be arranged so that one flows into another smoothly. They can also be set out in order of importance. A well-structured speech is like a chain, with one link fastened to the next. A speech written with this in mind will flow and put the audience at their ease. They will relax and so be able to concentrate more easily on what is being said.

Keep your message simple without appearing patronizing or condescending. Be direct, positive and to the point without any abruptness. The syntax can influence the way a speech is delivered, so write it in a warm manner that can be translated into cheerful speech. Add a little colour by telling a story. This can also help to re-engage flagging interest. It is a good standby prop, an important ingredient to add at a strategic place in a speech that may be rather dry. This can be a useful addition for business presentations. (See Chapter Eight for more information.)

Avoid overloading a speech with too much information as this can be difficult for an audience to retain. If there is a necessity to provide copious facts, figures or statistics, you can give handouts as appropriate, or as an addition to visual aids. Make a note of where you are going to use these.

When the second draft is completed, put it away in a drawer and forget it for a few days. Come back to it later and view it afresh. This is the time to edit your speech and delete unnecessary material. Remember that a short, well-structured speech is preferable to one that is longer but less memorable.

Tape-record your speech, listen to yourself objectively and criticize your format. This is also a good opportunity to time it and make any alterations in length or pace of delivery.

STARTING AND FINISHING – A REMINDER

The introduction to your speech is dealt with on pages 52–3. But it is worth mentioning that you may find it easier to write it last of all, since an introduction may spring more easily to mind once you have completed your written work. Reading through your material will provide mental pictures to guide you towards an opening. Remember, your opening remarks set the tone of your speech and the reaction you will get from the audience. The closing remarks round off the speech and bring your talk to a definite end. It's a bad idea to try to memorize your entire speech (and perhaps an impossibility), but if you memorize your opening comments you start without hesitation – this will give you confidence in your performance. Similarly, a memorized closing remark rounds off the speech and might even provide the cue for applause!

The final draft

By the time you reach this stage of written preparation, you will be familiar with your text. You may feel that on the day of the presentation you will be ready to read it aloud from your script. This can work if you are a well-practised speaker with the knack of being able to read aloud, with an easy relaxed manner, and on some occasions, such as business presentations (see Chapter Six) this may be appropriate or even necessary. But using notes may lead speakers to read mechanically, and may serve as a distraction if waved around and continuously reshuffled. Another drawback is that if the speaker is prone to nervous shakes, holding the notes will make them more obvious. You will need to recover your place on the sheet time and time again; the turning of the pages needs to be unobtrusive; and the contact with your audience is more difficult to maintain when you have the written word separating the listeners from you. However, for people who have to make many speeches or presentations, reading may be the only practical solution, and below are some tips to help you do this effectively.

TIPS FOR PREPARING A SPEECH TO READ

Use a black pen on white paper and keep the writing quite large. Or, if printing from the computer, use a large point size and double-line spacing.

Rewrite your second draft in phrases and group them by ideas or in pairs.

Provide a good space between each phrase. This avoids confusion and marks the end of one idea and the beginning of another. Writing out your speech in this way enables you to look at the audience regularly and then return to your place with comparative ease.

Write as you would speak and avoid the use of too may abstract concepts. Use pictorial language when the opportunity presents itself.

Prompt cards

However, there is another way. Many speakers transcribe the main topics of the material onto postcards. These are known as prompt cards. They enable you to refer to major points that will serve as cues during your delivery.

It can be hard to relinquish sheaves of paper that hold well-researched information in exchange for small rectangles of cardboard holding no more than a few headings. You may think you will never remember anything from them and the first time you attempt to rehearse your speech, your confidence can take a nosedive as you realize your worst fears.

This can be the danger period: the transition from paper to card – that reluctant surrendering of reassuring sheaves of rustling paper. Try to see this as a testing time and, if you can, persevere and use the cards. Once you make that breakthrough you will go from strength to strength.

Preparing prompt cards

If you decide to use cards, here are some suggestions for layout:

• Use one side of the card only.

• Number each one clearly with a black or coloured pen.

• List major points that need addressing, but resist the temptation to cram more than the essentials onto the postcard, or you may spend much of the speech peering at details that have been written in tiny handwriting.

• Insert any vital information that needs careful reference.

• The cards may be separate or strung together, whichever is the more comfortable.

Once you have done this, practise. That way you will improve and gain confidence. You will be able to look at the audience while you speak and communication will be at its strongest.

Here is a simple example of a prompt card from a father of the bride:

4.

Sarah growing up

Baby – pram story

At school – missing school report

As a teenager – party at our house

Familiarity breeds content! Once your notes have been pruned to postcard headings, rehearse your speech as often as you feel the need. (Chapter Four gives details about modulation skills to help your delivery.) Become familiar with your voice by monitoring it on a tape-recorder. This way you will receive quick, efficient feedback, and make any improvements needed.

As mentioned earlier, it is best to avoid the temptation of memorizing a speech. Some people will wish to do this as a back-up. However, it is much easier to forget lines than to forget the gist of what you wish to say. Forgetting a word or sentence can throw some people and thus undermine their confidence still further. Familiarizing is better than memorizing. It allows the speaker's personality to come into focus and the speech will sound more spontaneous than word-by-word rendering.

So, make a friend of your speech and have fun rehearsing! Remember that the key word is *practise*!

Giving impromptu speeches

For those well versed in the art of public speaking this may not be difficult; for the novice it can be nerve-wracking. Always be prepared for the unexpected. If you attend a number of social functions and think that you might at some stage be asked to 'fill in' (give a vote of thanks or a talk, or introduce a speaker), carry with you a blueprint or skeleton speech (with the key points on cards) that can be used in an emergency. This is particularly appropriate if you feel that you are not good at thinking on your feet.

Keep a notebook of amusing jokes and anecdotes (see Chapter Eight for ideas) or use the space at the end of this book. Practise rehearsing one or two of these from time to time. This will prepare you for that unexpected invitation.

There are two great tools, both of which have already been described, to support impromptu speeches: these are structure and storytelling.

Structure

The 'tell 'em' structure: Tell 'em what you're going to tell 'em, tell 'em, tell 'em what you've told 'em. When asked to make impromptu speeches, speakers can feel out of control if they have no framework within which to set their thoughts. The 'tell 'em' structure can be used in many situations, such as a corridor conversation, leaving someone a message on a phone, or standing up at short notice in front of a group.

In the example below, the job-leaver has a simple structure to keep them focused and prevent a rambling discourse.

Example: Impromptu speech by someone leaving a job

> *'Thank you so much for the leaving present, it was a very kind gesture. I'd like to say a few words about why leaving XYZ Advertising was such a difficult decision to make for three main reasons...the job itself, the clients and, last and most importantly, my great colleagues here. So why did I love the job?'...*

Storytelling

If you were part of a large group and were suddenly called upon to give a speech on France, it would seem daunting. What is difficult is that we have a lot of information in our head, but no planned format for its delivery. One way, as we have seen above, would be to use some structure, so that we could talk about the landscape, the people and the food and wine in order to give ourselves direction. The other alternative would be to tell a simple story about your experiences of the subject:

Example: Impromptu speech about France using storytelling

> *'To tell you a little about France I'd like to take you back to when I was 14 at school and embarked on a French exchange with Luc, a French boy of my own age, from Elbeuf in Normandy'...*

The well-planned and executed speech

One of the most famous speeches is 'I have a dream', given by Martin Luther King in Washington DC, on 28th August, 1963:

'I am happy to join with you today in what will go down in history as the greatest demonstration for freedom in the history of our nation.

Five score years ago, a great American, in whose symbolic shadow we stand today, signed the Emancipation Proclamation...

...But one hundred years later, the Negro still is not free. One

hundred years later, the life of the Negro is still sadly crippled by the manacles of segregation and the chains of discrimination. One hundred years later, the Negro lives on a lonely island of poverty in the midst of a vast ocean of material prosperity. One hundred years later, the Negro still languishes in the corners of American society and finds himself an exile in his own land.

So we've come here today to dramatize a shameful condition. In a sense, we've come to our nation's capital to cash a check. When the architects of our Republic wrote the magnificent words of the Constitution and the Declaration of Independence, they were signing a promissory note to which every American was to fall heir. This note was a promise that all men – yes, black men as well as white men – would be guaranteed the unalienable rights of life, liberty, and the pursuit of happiness.

It is obvious today that America has defaulted on this promissory note insofar as her citizens of color are concerned. Instead of honoring this sacred obligation, America has given the Negro people a bad check, a check which has come back marked 'insufficient funds'. But we refuse to believe that the bank of justice is bankrupt. We refuse to believe that there are insufficient funds in the great vaults of opportunity of this nation. So we've come to cash this check – a check that will give us upon demand the riches of freedom and the security of justice.

We have also come to this hallowed spot to remind America of the fierce urgency of 'now'. This is no time to engage in the luxury of cooling off or to take the tranquilizing drug of gradualism. Now is the time to make real the promises of democracy. Now is the time to rise from the dark and desolate valley of segregation to the sunlit path of racial justice. Now is the time to lift our nation from the quicksand of racial injustice to the solid rock of brotherhood. Now is the time to make justice a reality for all of God's children...

...There are those who are asking the devotees of civil rights: 'When will you be satisfied?' We can never be satisfied as long as the Negro is the victim of the unspeakable horrors of police brutality. We can never be satisfied as long as our bodies, heavy with the fatigue of travel, cannot gain lodging in the motels of the highways and the hotels of the cities. We cannot be satisfied as long as the Negro's basic mobility is from a smaller ghetto to a larger one. We can never be satisfied as long as our children are stripped of their selfhood and robbed of their dignity by signs stating 'For Whites Only'. We cannot be satisfied as long as a Negro in Mississippi cannot vote and a Negro in New York believes he has nothing for which to vote. No, no, we are not satisfied, and we will not be satisfied until justice rolls down like waters and righteousness like a mighty stream!...

...Go back to Mississippi, go back to Alabama, go back to South Carolina, go back to Georgia, go back to Louisiana, go back to the slums and ghettos of our Northern cities, knowing that somehow this situation can and will be changed. Let us not wallow in the valley of despair....

...I have a dream that one day this nation will rise up and live out the true meaning of its creed: 'We hold these truths to be self-evident; that all men are created equal.'

I have a dream that one day on the red hills of Georgia the sons of former slaves and the sons of former slave owners will be able to sit down together at the table of brotherhood. I have a dream that one day even the state of Mississippi, a state sweltering with the heat of injustice, sweltering with the heat of oppression, will be transformed into an oasis of freedom and justice.

I have a dream that my four little children will one day live in a nation where they will not be judged by the color of their skin but by the content of their character.

I have a dream today!

I have a dream that one day, down in Alabama, with its vicious racists, with its governor having his lips dripping with the words of interposition and nullification, one day right there in Alabama little black boys and black girls will be able to join hands with little white boys and white girls as sisters and brothers...I have a dream today!

I have a dream that one day every valley shall be exalted, every hill and mountain shall be made low, the rough places will be made plain and the crooked places will be made straight, and the glory of the Lord shall be revealed, and all flesh shall see it together!...

...So let freedom ring! From the prodigious hilltops of New Hampshire, let freedom ring. From the mighty mountains of New York, let freedom ring, from the heightening Alleghenies of Pennsylvania! Let freedom ring from the snowcapped Rockies of Colorado! Let freedom ring from the curvaceous slopes of California! But not only that.

Let freedom ring from Stone Mountain of Georgia! Let freedom ring from Lookout Mountain in Tennessee! Let freedom ring from every hill and mole hill of Mississippi. From every mountainside, let freedom ring, and when this happens...when we allow freedom to ring, when we let it ring from every village and every hamlet, from every state and every city, we will be able to speed up that day when all of God's children, black men and white men, Jews and Gentiles, Protestants and Catholics, will be able to join hands and sing in the words of the old Negro spiritual: 'Free at last! Free at last! Thank God Almighty, we are free at last!''

What points can we learn from this speech that we can employ when speechmaking?

The use of a story as an engagement item:
The Emancipation Proclamation.

The use of a storytelling allegory:
'America has given the Negro people a bad check...'

The use of repetition:
'One hundred years later...' four times
'Now is the time...' four times.
'We cannot/we can never' five times.
'Go back to' six times.
'I have a dream' seven times.
'Let freedom ring' nine times.

Delivery:
King's delivery of the speech was outstanding. He ensured that how he spoke the words was at least as powerful as the words themselves by employing changing volume, projection and emphasis.

The badly planned and executed speech

There are certain things that you should always avoid saying when giving a speech, that will give offence, show your lack of preparation and generally make you look unprofessional.

'Ladies and gentlemen, this is the fifth time I've done this speech in the last month so it's becoming quite automatic now. I realize that the subject is very boring, so I'll start off with a funny joke I heard recently... have you heard the one about the Irishman, the woman secretary and the homosexual?...'

'I've got about 45 slides to run through in the next hour and as I got here a little late we'd better get going...does anyone know how to connect my computer to the projector?...'

'I realize that you won't be able to read this slide at the back of the room as it is a very busy slide, but I thought it might give you an idea of the complexity we're dealing with...'

'Here is a graph showing the ISJ growth amongst the KLA population. I'm not sure of the exact source of the data, but it gives you a general idea... What? You can't hear? Well, move a bit closer to the front then...'

'Unfortunately, we appear to have overrun by quarter of an hour so we'd better finish there. Actually, there is one last point; let's just take a final 10 minutes to talk it through...'

'I realize I've gone 30 minutes over time, but I hope you will all agree it was worth it. Any questions? No? Thank you.'

What can we learn from this speech?

- **Preparation:** Use structure in your presentation to ensure that you have a beginning, a middle and an end, and avoid throwing in additional issues at the end, having forgotten them earlier.

- Rehearse to ensure that you stick to your timings.

- Make sure you have practised with the audiovisual equipment and understand how it all works.

- **Content:** Know the sources of your reference material.

- Don't apologize for being there or for the nature of your content. See The Top 10 Phrases to Avoid, below.

- Don't use inappropriate humour.

- Engagement items should be relevant. (See page 54.)

- Don't use acronyms or abbreviations unless you are 100% sure that they will be understood by your audience.

- **Delivery:** Make sure you can be heard.

- **Visual aids:** Ensure that they can be seen and that you don't have too many.

But it's not always logistics, visual aids or preparation that make a poor speech. Sometimes it is choosing the wrong occasion, at the wrong time, with the wrong words.

Michael Moore's Oscar acceptance for the Academy Award for Best Documentary Feature in 2003 is a good example of this.

'...We like nonfiction, yet we live in fictitious times. We live in a time where we have fictitious election results that elect a fictitious president. We live in a time where we have a man sending us to war for fictitious reasons. Whether it's the fiction of duct tape, or the fiction of orange alerts. We are against this war, Mr Bush. Shame on you, Mr Bush, shame on you. And any time you get the Pope and the Dixie Chicks against you, your time is up. Thank you very much.'

The speech might have succeeded or have been well received by other audiences. However, Moore had failed to understand the mood and likely response of the audience at the Oscars. Consequently, the speech crashed.

THE TOP 10 PHRASES TO AVOID:

1. 'Ummm, errrr...'
2. 'Unaccustomed as I am...'
3. 'This is going to be pretty boring/dry I'm afraid...'
4. 'Sorry to take up your time...'
5. 'I'm very nervous about this...'
6. 'This is probably too simple/complicated for you...'
7. 'This is a busy slide...'
8. 'You won't be able to see this but....'
9. 'I'll read this slide out for you...'
10. 'I've included some extra slides for your interest...'

SUMMARY OF WRITING YOUR SPEECH

Begin research in advance and research facts to ensure accuracy.

Avoid overloading with excessive amounts of information.

Cut unnecessary padding. Aim to be economical.

Look for appropriate places that you can add light relief. (Jokes, quotations and definitions can be found in Chapter Eight.)

Be listener-orientated. Write to speak.

Be simple and direct – speak in a way the audience understands.

Write under four or five headings and, if necessary, sub-headings.

Have a clear, energetic and purposeful introduction.

Use reiteration where necessary, particularly in summing up.

Write several drafts so that you can edit and re-edit.

Transfer the main points of your speech to cards, or rewrite in phrases.

Mark where visual aids will be introduced.

Time the speech.

PRACTISE.

speechmakers' bible

chapter 4

Preparing and practising your delivery

'Speak clearly, if you speak at all; carve every
word before you let it fall.'
*Oliver Wendell Holmes, 19th century American
author and physician*

I f we were to ask most audience members to remember a boring speaker and then tell us what made it boring, many would immediately indicate that the speaker's voice had been 'monotonous'. The voice is a particularly important delivery skill for a speaker, particularly when needing to hold the attention of larger audiences over long periods of time.

So, the better your delivery, the better your speech. If you get your delivery perfected, your speech, whether for an informal or formal occasion, will have impact.

Modulation

Tone and pitch are important ways in which to add variety to the voice and some people are equipped with more natural range than others. However, those people without a wide natural range of pitch need not despair. There are several other ways in which a speaker can vary their voice to be most effective. This is known as modulation. Modulation is the use of expressive delivery. It can be thought of as having four elements: pause, pace, power and pitch.

Pause: Stopping occasionally to add impact or emphasis, or to allow your audience to digest what has just been said.

Pace: The pace sets the mood for the speech, be it rapid and exciting or slow, measured, conservative and in control.

Power: The combination of volume and projection as sound is generated from the stomach.

Pitch: The key in which we speak, also known as tone. Where your vocal range allows it, these should be set according to the mood you wish to create.

Speakers who have had feedback that their delivery is monotone, or suspect as much, should employ a combination of the other three elements of modulation in order to maximize their ability to communicate effectively with audiences.

Pause

To learn how to make effective use of the pause, before you start to speak, stop! Here's why:

- A pause establishes your presence.

- It gives you status.

- The audience has time to look you over.

- It gives them a chance to settle down.

- It gives you a chance to be heard from word one!

- If you begin your speech immediately, without waiting for complete quiet, you lose impact. Impact is vital!

- Pause between paragraphs and changes of thought. This aids clarity and helps the audience absorb what has been said.

Pause and emphasis

While it is valuable to lay stress on principal words, raising the volume may not prove effective. Here are some techniques that may be used to give emphasis, along with the pause.

Pronouns and adverbs are emphasized in cases of comparisons. Avoid over-emphasis when using conjunctions, articles, prepositions and subordinate words. For example:

Incorrect emphasis

In the beginning *was* the Word, and the Word was *with* God. And the Word *was* God.

Suggested emphasis

In the beginning was the *Word*, and the Word was with *God*. And the Word was *God*. (St John, Chapter 1)

Language needs to flow. If you speak it rhythmically, the sounds and messages will fall happily on the ears of listeners. Be selective when emphasizing words or statements and remember:

'I PAUSE AND I THINK.'
'I PAUSE AND YOU THINK.

Words lead from thoughts!

Relate sincerely with your audience. Let them see that you care about what you are saying. Allow your own personality to shine through. While you pause to think, the audience has space to process what has been said.

However, while natural use of both pause and emphasis is effective, remember that the over-use of both can be boring and affected.

EXERCISE 26
PAUSE AND EMPHASIS

The strokes indicate where you may pause. Highlighted words are in italics.

Pausing before and after the highlighted word:

The rain in Spain falls / *mainly* / **on the plain**.

You can bring down the volume and speak more slowly on the phrase you wish to emphasize:

The rain in Spain falls / *mainly on the plain.*
('Mainly on the plain' is spoken more quietly than the rest of the sentence.)

You can slightly elongate the highlighted word for emphasis. In this instance you may not wish to use pause:

The rain in Spain falls *m-a-i-n-l-y on the plain.*

Pace

It is important to regulate the passage of your speech. Avoid the tendency to speak at one rate throughout, either too fast or too slow. Never rush.

Pace is varied rate. It is the adjustment of words and phrases within a speech. Consequently, pace is closely linked with pause.

Remember to:

- Breathe easily from your centre to help alleviate tension.
- Use pauses between sentences and paragraphs and for effect.

Towards the end of the talk, slow down the delivery to allow the audience time to realize that you are drawing to a close.

Never fade out by weakening the voice. Keep it strong and sure.

 **EXERCISE 27**
MONITORING THE PACE

Practise reading passages from a book or magazine. Listen to yourself on a tape-recorder to help you monitor your pace. Look for places where it can be varied. Ask yourself the following questions:

- What is the mood of the passage?

- At what points should I slow down or speed up?
  - To clarify a point or statement – slow down.
  - To help build a state of suspense – start slowly and then gain momentum by speeding up.
  - To pass over the less important features of the speech – speed up.

- Am I speaking clearly in the faster passages?

- Mood is a very important ingredient. Like the weather and temperature, it can change very quickly. Use those changes to add excitement, colour and depth to your work.

Power

Power is the volume, the energy behind the voice. It is the reinforcement of sound.

This is made possible by the use of the resonators and the breathing muscles. If we allow our outgoing breath to pass over the vocal chords in a positive, well-directed and steady stream of air, we can enlarge our sound. The more air pressure produced when breathing out, the louder the sound will be.

When you speak to an audience, the amount of power you need in your voice will depend on the size and acoustics of the room or hall. It is useful therefore to know beforehand about the venue. (See also Chapter Five.)

Remember that as you do the following exercise you will require good postural alignment, so that there is physical support and space in the throat and chest for breath. To help achieve this, place your hand on the midriff, and imagine sound as well as breath coming from your middle. This will enable your throat to feel free and open. Focus on what you are saying, and open your mouth for the words. This will help energize the sound and power of your voice. Aim for fullness of tone. Avoid shouting or straining from the throat.

EXERCISE 28
POWER AND PROJECTION 1

Using your largest room, choose an object near to you and make that your focal point. Speak the following sentence quietly and distinctly:

My message is clear.

Now move away from this point a couple of paces and repeat the sentence, slightly increasing your volume.

My message is clear.

When you are some distance from your starting point, change your sentence to:

My message is loud and clear.

EXERCISE 29
POWER AND PROJECTION 2

Now do the same with the following:

Good morning, everyone.

I call the meeting to order.

Quiet, ladies and gentlemen!
The play is about to begin.

EXERCISE 30
VARYING THE VOLUME

Vary your voice according to the content of the following passage. Clarity of speech is vital, particularly when speaking the quieter portions. Avoid a fading-out of the voice.

The house you visit is a house of history. So pause awhile in our great hall. Absorb the atmosphere and quiet of this place.

Now view the tapestry; admire the craft. A needlework measured out in tiny stitches, which when completed tells of one enormous, bloody war. See, compacted in this weave, how combat sought political resolve.

Pitch

Pitch is the key in which we speak. In speech there are high, middle and low pitches.

When we speak, our various pitches tend to merge into one another and are dependent on the mood and the meaning of our speech. This is illustrated as follows:

High pitch
This is used in moments of exhilaration, excitement or happiness.

Middle pitch
This is used for general conversation and moderate speech.

Low pitch
This is used for sad and solemn speech.

Exercise and vary your pitch. It will enhance vocal expression and augment platform presence. Practise reading a fairy tale aloud. Imagine you have children as your audience. Make use of pause, emphasis, pace, volume and intensity. Decide the various moods of the passage and foster the different pitches to suit them.

Remember that with each new paragraph, the voice needs to be refreshed; so raise your pitch at the beginning slightly. This revives interest.

Intensity

Intensity is the pizzazz, the zing, zip, wallop of your speech! It is the sparkle behind your voice. Intensity is the life force – the energy and enthusiasm you inject into your manner and voice.

Vocally, it includes pause and emphasis, pace, pitch and power, with the added ingredients of sincerity, humour and goodwill.

Spiritually, it includes belief in your message and total involvement. So:

ATTACK YOUR SPEECH WITH ANIMATION AND DRIVE!

Give your audience mental shocks

While a speaker may appear to have a few fascinated listeners gazing up at the platform, this is not in itself proof that the listeners are riveted by his or her utterances! An attentive face may be concealing completely different thoughts: perhaps puzzling over the next meeting at the office, or whether or not they had remembered to lock the back door!

By stimulating the audience through modulation, the speaker keeps them alert. They will not have time to be distracted.

PASSAGES FOR SPEAKING PRACTICE

The following passages are for practice. Before you read them aloud, look again at:

Mood

The mood of a passage helps determine the way in which it is delivered. It is, therefore, important to establish this at the outset.

Breath pauses

Go through a passage and mark breaks for supplementary breaths, at full stops and the ends of paragraphs.

Pace

Look for where the pace might be varied. Be guided by content.

Pitch

Vary the key of your voice in accordance with mood and material.

Emphasis

Stress important words, those used to make a comparison, and words that add colour. Avoid being too emphatic, as this can destroy the flow.

Power and intensity

The volume of a passage will be dependent on mood. Increasing power by degrees can help build a feeling of suspense and climax. Speaking quietly can also create atmosphere, and is a most effective way of highlighting important material. Remember to speak with energy and involvement.

Pause

Having established where you are going to take your breaks at full stops, some commas, between paragraphs and with changes of thought, there may also be places where pause can be used to create effect. Knowing how long to pause develops with experience. Never milk a pause for its own sake, but rather use with discretion – mindful of the needs of your audience.

EXERCISE 31
FRIENDS

Harry Trafford rushed onto the platform just as his train drew out of the little country station. He watched it as it disappeared from view. Resignedly, Harry put his suitcase down. He shivered. This was not the kind of weather to hang about outside in.

For some time Harry sat there, trying to ignore the sharp February chill that furtively seeped through his body. He gave an involuntary shudder – the next train was not due for another two hours. What on earth was he to do in the meantime? Apart from the station master, the place was deserted. It was then he heard footsteps behind him. They stopped just by his suitcase. Harry viewed a very expensive pair of brogues.

'Harry! Harry Trafford! What on earth are you doing in this neck of the woods?'

Harry looked up from his low vantage point.

'Ken? I can't believe it! Of all the places to bump into you!'

Harry jumped to his feet, and grasped Ken by the hand. His face beamed. Ken laughed. 'I live just round the corner. Dropped by to book my ticket to town for tomorrow morning. Thought I'd avoid the rush! Believe it or not, we're quite busy here early mornings. Look, there's my local across the road. Shall we go and sink a few pints for old times' sake?'

Harry picked up his case. 'Let's do just that!'

EXERCISE 32
THE HAT BOX

Travelling on the underground
From Waterloo to Charing Cross.
Directly opposite me
A woman sits,
With hat box
Resting on her knee.
Inscrutable – expressionless
She stares ahead, a world apart.
Hand gently rests upon her charge,
Black striped box
Bound with string,
Hexagonal and large.

Perhaps her wedding veil it holds,
Or picture hat in white tissue.
A dimpled grotto of delight,
Shop-smelling, luscious, new.

At Charing Cross we leave the train
To go our separate ways.
She with hat box held aloft,
And I go home to Hayes.

EXERCISE 33
THE CLOCK

The Victorian grandfather clock stopped at 4am on the 21st of November, 1965. It stopped the moment that Richard's father died. He would've liked to have sold it then, but instead, he compromised by not resetting the hands.

The clock now stood estranged, gathering dust in a darkened corner of the landing. When Richard went to bed, he sometimes forgot to switch on the upstairs lights, and occasionally fancied that the grandfather clock took on the appearance of a person standing in shadow; standing and waiting.

Then, on the first anniversary of his father's death, at 4am precisely, the clock struck the hour. It resounded almost defiantly throughout the house. The chimes penetrated Richard's dream. He started awake and rushed out of his bedroom and onto the landing, shaking from the fright, but the last note was now dying on the air. The clock nursed its seal of secrecy.

Richard didn't sleep again that night, and next morning he restarted the clock. He reset the hands and wound it with the key his father had used. Listening to the familiar tick, he felt surprisingly reassured. He polished the wood and some of its former glory was restored, although it was still darkened by shadow. Richard switched on the landing light. It was as though he saw the clock for the first time. He smiled: 'I hadn't noticed before what a handsome face you have.' (His father had been handsome.) 'I think I'll go out this morning and buy a spotlight. You need to be seen, old chap! Why didn't I think of that before?'

Speaking dialogue

Use this passage to practise dialogue. Vary your pitch level to establish the different characters. The mood needs to be light and the dialogue quick on cues. Keep up the pace and discover where you can use pause to good effect.

EXERCISE 34
LOVE'S TREASURE

Henry Price, romantic novelist, living on the outskirts of Weston-super-Mare, opened the front door of his house one morning last June, and found himself face to face with the beautiful Angela Culpepper.

'I've come about the job.'

'Job?'

'Yes, your advert – in the paper. I rang – you asked me to come.'

'Oh yes. Yes, of course. Miss er...'

'Culpepper. But you can call me Angela if you like.'

'Follow me, Angela, and turn right. Mind the step. Here we are. This is the study where I work. A bit cramped, I'm afraid – never managed to acquire a decent one. Take a seat, won't you? I'll just move these papers – clear the decks so to speak. Oh, get off there, you stupid animal – Shoo! Out you go!' A tortoiseshell cat leapt off a pile of books, causing a lamp shade to sway precariously on its stand.

'Now then, I'd like to take one or two details if I may. I'll just get my notebook if I can find it under all the paperwork.'

'Here's your notebook.' Angela's smile as she handed it to him so fascinated Henry, that he could only stare. She couldn't be more than twenty-four or so, he thought. Tall, slim, skin the colour of ivory, milky-blue eyes, chestnut hair that caught the light when she moved her head. Oh, but she was lovely. Yes, he could see her fitting perfectly into his next novel.

Creating beautiful women was part of Henry's job as a writer. In the past it had afforded him a great deal of pleasure. Now, at sixty-four, his inventive powers were beginning to wane and while his income allowed him and his wife to live out their days in relative comfort, Henry needed fresh stimulus to revive his old writing skills.

'Anything the matter, Mr Price?'

'No, no, it was nothing, nothing at all. Well, as you may know, I'm an author. Have you heard of me?' Henry shot Angela an uncertain glance.

'No, I don't read very much.'

'Ah well, no matter. I write romantic fiction. At present I'm in the process of finishing the final draft of *Love's Treasure*.

Now what I need is someone such as yourself to type the manuscript for me. Not too worried about speed, but must be accurate, you understand. You do touch-type?'

'Yes.'

'Good, very good.' (Those eyes! He must concentrate, damn it.) 'Cash in hand as advertised – flexi-hours – two or three mornings a week. Will you accept the job?' Henry held his breath.

'Yes. Thank you very much. I'd like to accept.'

'Next Monday suit you?'

'Yes.'

'Then Monday it is.'

'Freda,' he said to his wife later that morning, 'she's perfect, quite perfect.'

SUMMARY: PREPARING AND PRACTISING YOUR DELIVERY

Make your speech more expressive by incorporating pauses at appropriate moments.

Vary the pace, volume and tone at which you speak to stop your voice from becoming monotonous and sending the audience to sleep.

Check that you are putting emphasis on the right words.

Check that you aren't speaking too slowly or too quickly.

Tape yourself speaking and listen back, or ask a friend to listen to you and then be honest with their criticism.

Be enthusiastic in your delivery – if you sound energetic and excited about your topic, this will transfer to the audience.

PRACTISE.

speechmakers' bible

chapter 5

Giving your speech or presentation

In Chapter Four we looked at just one of the delivery skills involved in making a speech or presentation: the use of the voice. Voice is, of course, important, but in this chapter we will look at the importance of other elements involved, such as dress rehearsal, gestures and last checks to ensure a faultless performance.

Experiments conducted have suggested that words could account for as little as 7% of the impression created, compared with 93% made by the nonverbal communication and how the voice was used. It is therefore vital that speakers not only master the 'what' of preparing and planning excellent structure, words, content and visual aids, but also the 'how' of optimizing the use of their voice, gestures, movement and eye contact with the audience to maximize the effectiveness of how you present.

Communicate with the programme organizer

Your speech has been written, your cards are prepared, your visual aids, if you are using them, are assembled. It is now useful to acquire some information about the place in which you are to speak. Whether this is a social or business occasion, here are some questions you might ask:

• How many people will be in the audience?

• How many speakers are there going to be?

- How long should my speech last?

- Will the chairperson or organizer write a brief initial introduction about me, or should I prepare one beforehand?

- What is the size of the room in which I will speak?

- Will I be required to speak at a lectern?

- Will there be a microphone? A projector?

- Will I be standing on a raised platform or on a level with the audience?

Know the venue and the seating arrangements

If the room is large and the seats are arranged in theatre style, you will need to throw your voice to the back of the hall. Acoustics will also affect carrying power. So, if there is an opportunity, practise a few sentences for sound level before the event. If speaking to a very large audience for any length of time, some form of amplification will be required.

When the room is arranged horseshoe fashion, the audience will be much smaller: fifteen to twenty people. This can be an ideal setting, because it encourages rapport within the group. Also the speaker can move easily among them.

Request your needs

If you are the sole speaker, politely expressing your wishes
will help you to prepare with confidence. For example, if it
is to be a small grouped audience and you like the idea of
arranging the seats in a horseshoe fashion, send in a
diagram suggesting this.

Will you be introduced?

If there is a chairperson in charge, ask whether or not you as
the speaker will be introduced to the audience. As a good
deal of time and effort will have gone into the talk, you will
deserve a decent build-up.

You may like to write your own initial introduction and send
it ahead to the chairperson. Give some local background on
yourself: your achievements and interests. Keep it short.

If you are to be introduced, you may wish to thank the person
who has introduced you, or acknowledge certain people
present (the chairperson or president and the audience)
before beginning your speech.

Take time for a dress rehearsal.

Rehearsal is one part of giving a speech that we all know we
should do, but with alarming regularity, don't do. Personal
discomfort with rehearsing causes us to find any excuse not
to do it, usually: 'I didn't have enough time.' This excuse is

usually rendered all the more unbelievable considering the time spent instead on creating too many overcomplicated and irrelevant visual aids. Rehearsal should be considered our number one ally in the effort to give a great speech. But why?

Familiarity with your content: It's all too obvious when someone is presenting something they haven't seen before or are unfamiliar with since a whole gamut of clues give away their surprise as the next visual is revealed.

Familiarity with any equipment: If only all audiovisual equipment were simple and worked first time. By rehearsing we become familiar with controls, switches, how to plug and start various devices and, just as importantly, how to switch them off!

Familiarity with visual aids: A common error is to print out a set of visuals and merely read them on the train home. Not running through them live means we don't become familiar with any builds (see Chapter Two) and effects, or other functionality that we just won't know from print-outs.

Familiarity with your co-speakers in team presentations or when you are one of a series of speakers: In order to appear as a team when presenting, it's vital to have smooth and effective handovers. Your part of the speech commences when you're introduced and doesn't finish until you've made a good job of introducing the next speaker and exiting from the stage. As we will look at later in Chapter Six, it is also important that you rehearse effective question handling across the team. An embarrassing situation arises when you don't actually know who your other presenters are!

Timings: The time it takes you to read through your materials has little bearing on how long in reality it will take you to give the speech. Think of the longest time you could imagine it taking and double it and you'll be in the right area.

Ability to find and articulate the right word: Sometimes when we read through our materials it all makes sense, but when we try to say it we can't find the right word or become tongue twisted and are unable to say it. Only by rehearsing out loud will you discover which words are going to trip you up.

Rehearsal techniques

The rehearsal should be made as realistic as possible. Below are listed a number of different techniques for rehearsal, in order of their effectiveness:

Highly effective
Full dress rehearsal in the room with the audiovisuals and some mock audience members asking questions and giving you feedback.

Full dress rehearsal in the room with the audiovisuals and some mock audience members giving you feedback.

Full dress rehearsal in the room with the audiovisuals and some mock audience members.

Moderately effective
Full dress rehearsal in the room with the audiovisuals but no mock audience.

Full dress rehearsal in a different room with the audiovisuals and some mock audience members giving you feedback.

Full dress rehearsal in a different room with the audiovisuals and some mock audience members but no feedback.

Effective
Full dress rehearsal in a different room with the audiovisuals but no mock audience.

Full dress rehearsal in the room and some mock audience members asking questions and giving you feedback, but without the audiovisuals.

Rehearsal without audiovisuals, but with the benefit of some mock audience members.

Better than nothing
Rehearsal in front of mirror, timing yourself.
Rehearsal in the car or on a walk.
Full rehearsal of just the beginning and the end.

Ineffective
No rehearsal.

Reading through visuals in your own mind.

The key point for rehearsals is that they should be as similar to the actual live event as you can make them. If you are speaking with other people, don't accept their excuses for why they can't make the rehearsal, they'll thank you in the end!

The lighting

A speaker needs to be well lit on all sides. Make sure there will not be lights shining into your eyes.

The microphone

Just because you are presented with a microphone doesn't mean you are obliged to use it. It may be there just as a precaution and, if the room and audience are small enough, it may be easier and more effective to use your normal un-amplified voice. Larger audiences and rooms necessitate the use of microphones.

TOP TIPS ON USING MICROPHONES:

Familiarize yourself with the mike. What type is it? If it is on a stand can you remove it? If not, is it at the correct height for you to start talking without fumbling around with it? If it is a podium mike, can you get a clip mike? How does it switch on and off? Is there a spare if this one stops working?

Always maintain a constant distance between your mike and your mouth. This is more difficult with podium mikes, but clip mikes work well. If using a hand mike, rest the hand holding the mike lightly against your body to anchor it there and maintain a good speaking distance. Most mikes work best at an operating distance of about six inches away from your mouth, but always test it out.

Soldiers say 'a rifle is always loaded' in order to avoid accidents and always err on the side of safety. A similar rule applies with microphones: 'a microphone is always on'. Modern microphones are very sensitive and may pick up comments you don't intend the audience to hear.

People associate confidence with a head-up posture. Bring the mike up to your head and not vice-versa.

Avoid feedback: Make sure you have tested the volume of the mike and adjusted it against feedback. Testing where you are going to speak is essential as the system might be fine when tested in one part of the room, but may go haywire when you take to the stage next to a loudspeaker.

Using autocues

Most television presenters are so skilled in the use of autocues that the viewers can hardly tell they are using them. This could lull the novice public speaker into thinking autocues represent a short cut to accomplished conference speaking. However, they can make people appear mechanical and detached. The following tips will help guide you through their use:

Challenge whether you have to use one: Just because the technology exists doesn't mean it has to be used. Speakers are normally at their most engaging when talking naturally to the audience. The autocue tends to make people read and stay fixed to a spot. Ask if you can be 'set free' to use your notes or operate in the way you are most comfortable with.

Position the autocue appropriately: A common error is to accept the positioning of the screen where it has been set up for you, even if it appears as though you are staring at the floor or away from the audience. Position the screen so that it seems as if you are looking at a part of the audience when using it.

Use more than one screen: If you are provided with two or three screens in different positions, swap between them. It will seem as if you are establishing eye contact with different groups of people. If you need to make an important point, take the time to look away from the autocue to the heart of the audience and speak directly and naturally to them.

Rehearse, rehearse and rehearse again: When you use an autocue, practise at least three full run-throughs with the equipment. The autocue will have an operator that advances the text. Insist that you rehearse with the operator who will be supporting you in the live performance. In that way they will get used to your tempo, when you speed up and slow down and the times you may pause or stop for questions.

You drive the speed: There is a tendency when using the autocue to speak progressively faster so you don't get left behind by the text. It is the operator's job to go at your speed. When you get to the venue, talk things through with your operator, take your time and stop or pause when you need to.

To sum up, autocues are only worth using if your delivery remains natural. Practise until you are so comfortable with the equipment that you are able to focus on how well you're engaging with the audience...just like a newsreader.

Avoiding common mistakes

When it comes to speeches and presentations, remember that first impressions count, so it's vital to avoid a negative initial impact. Many speakers have lost their audiences within the first five minutes by falling into some common traps:

Being late: Never keep your audience waiting. In business it's unprofessional, for a social speech it's just plain rude.

Starting your speech when people aren't listening: It takes audiences a while to settle and stop thinking about other things. Don't start until they are all ready to listen.

Bad jokes: Probably the worst start to a speech or presentation is the inappropriate or badly delivered joke or 'humorous' story. Unfortunately for the majority of us, the percentage of the population who are actually good at telling jokes is tiny; however, many ill-informed speakers appear to be ignorant of that fact and persevere with poorly delivered efforts. Inappropriate jokes are usually due to a lack of understanding of the audience and how to pitch to their level. The classic example of this is the over-the-top best man's speech or sexist humour in a modern work setting. If you're unsure whether a joke will work, play on the safe side and forget about it.

Negative body language: Although we may not be sure exactly what tells us the speaker is nervous, we can always 'smell the fear'. The speaker will shuffle to the front, with his orher head held low and shoulders rounded, failing to make eye contact with any of the audience. Frequently they sway nervously from side to side.

Not speaking loudly enough: Inexperienced or more timid speakers have a tendency to speak too quietly, prompting a cry of 'speak up' or 'we can't hear you' from the audience. When preparing, get someone to stand at the back of the venue and see if they can hear you.

Lack of desire to be there: Audiences are good at reading your desire to be there. It could be that you are bored, having done the same speech a hundred times or you just want to be somewhere else. Either way it's vital to embody positive intent and make the audience feel important.

Apologizing for being there: This early act of submissiveness establishes that you are likely to waste the audience's time.

Audiovisual support equipment not working: Business presentations are frequently supported by complex audiovisual support equipment. Lack of preparation often leads to projectors not working, Powerpoint presentations not opening and dodgy microphones. All these leave audiences with the impression that things are going to go downhill rapidly.

Gestures

Too many gestures can be distracting, however well thought out, so use these economically. If you will be holding cards or notes, practise beforehand the gestures you wish to make.

Remember:

- The gesture slightly precedes the word.

- Try not to lean while making gestures.

- Keep eyes raised.

- Arm movements should be large enough to be seen. Make them from the waist with firmness and flow.

Gestures made in the course of everyday life are natural, spontaneous movements, expressing an attitude of mind. They may arise from emotional feeling, or they may be used to express an idea, illustrate a point, or reinforce an argument.

Unfortunately, when we are on show, either acting or giving a speech, our dialogue, however well intended or felt, is not entirely natural. It has been rehearsed. In addition, we can become acutely self-aware and, while consciousness of self is essential, overt self-consciousness can result in tensions that promote graceless, staccato movements and gestures, undermining the speaker and acting as a distraction.

Discipline your gestures by learning to stand or sit still. It is irritating to watch a speaker sway from side to side, or pace up and down on a platform like a trapped animal. Initially and most importantly, learn the art of repose. If, while making a speech, you are using cards on which are written key points, hold these just below chest level so that you are able to look at your audience, and speak out. This has now given you something to do with your hands. If you need to use an arm movement, your right or left hand is available to do so. Stand with your legs slightly apart, with the weight evenly distributed on both feet. This 'grounds' you, and may act as a reminder to keep still.

Let your thoughts guide your movements, and remember that they need to be allied with facial and vocal expression.

Avoiding irritating habits

Repetitive movements or sounds are thrown into high relief when speaking in front of a group of people. Some habits to avoid are:

- 'uhhs' and 'uhmms'

- short coughs or sniffs

- smacking the lips

- biting the lips

- touching the ear or nose

- repeated adjustment of spectacles

- scratching the head

- fiddling with necktie or necklace

- swaying from side to side

- pacing up and down like an animal in captivity

- looking downwards too much instead of at the audience

Asking someone to video you will probably seem very daunting, but if you get the chance you will be able to monitor any habits.

What should I do with my hands?

If you are using prompt cards, hold these with both hands, just below chest level. If you want to make a gesture, your right or left hand can be used. This looks good and prevents unnecessary fidgeting. Avoid placing one hand in your pocket while holding the cards in the other: it looks slovenly and, particularly for the business environment, unprofessional.

When cards are not being used, avoid crossing your arms, but adopt a position that is comfortable for you. One arm may rest in front of you at waist level, and the other down at your side. Later, during your speech, the two arms can remain at your side. Alternatively, your arms may be placed in front of you, one hand resting on the other. Some people like to stand with their arms held behind their back. All these postures are acceptable, but varying them throughout your speech will create a more relaxed and confident look.

Checking your appearance

Aim at being comfortable and smart. Fashion is changing all the time, so the suggestions given here are guidelines only:

For the woman

As the main source of focus will be on the face, pay special attention to make-up if you wear it. Strong lighting drains natural colour, so it's a good idea to apply blusher and emphasize the lips and the eyes.

Keep the hair away from the face, so that it is not masked, but retain a soft style.

Earrings can soften the face and add interest, but avoid the large, dangling variety: they will be a distraction.

A colourful scarf or brooch adds a touch of sophistication and interest to the neckline.

Avoid wearing dull colours unless they are offset by something bright and cheerful, such as a scarf. Red is a strong, dramatic hue, and providing it doesn't drain colour from the face, can create impact. Avoid busy patterns. They are too tiring on the eye.

Check that your hemlines are straight, especially if wearing a full skirt, as these sometimes have a tendency to dip.

For the man

Wear a well-fitting suit and a shirt with the cuffs just showing below the jacket. The tie should be neatly tied.

Black shoes are preferable to brown: brown tends to distract the eye. Dark-coloured socks should be worn, rather than white. Make sure the socks cover the calves adequately.

For the less formal occasion, smart casual may be worn.

Smile please!

Even, white teeth are cosmetic assets but not everyone is blessed with a perfect set of these. Some speakers are afraid to smile, because of their imperfect teeth. The hand goes up to the mouth, or the expression remains solemn in order to hide the teeth. If this is the case with you, in addition to making your own routine check-ups, either get your teeth fixed by the dentist, or make up your mind to forget about them and be yourself. The confident person will smile anyway!

How are you feeling?

Nervous reactions can inhibit hunger pangs, so that while we don't think we are hungry, our stomachs may tell us otherwise and protest by rumbling. This can be a source of embarrassment. If you think this may happen to you, eat a little food containing complex carbohydrates, such as a fresh banana (not over-ripe) or nuts, prior to your speech.

If this is an after-dinner speech, or another social occasion, monitor your alcohol consumption. A drunken speaker is embarrassing (and indeed insulting to your host or guest of honour). From your own point of view, even being slightly tipsy, particularly if you've never spoken in public before, will make you feel less in control and lacking in confidence.

Quietly does it

Before giving a speech for a social occasion, leave yourself plenty of time on the day to prepare. You may like to rehearse your speech once more, and then save your voice as much as possible. Conserve your energy and you will remain calmer than if you rush about or engage in unnecessary chat. Avoid wearing yourself out before making your speech.

Listen while you wait

If you are one of several speakers waiting their turn, focus on what your fellow speakers are saying. It rehearses your powers of concentration and temporarily directs attention away from yourself. This may help alleviate feelings of nervousness.

Speak out

When using prompt cards or sheets of paper for notes, ensure they are held just below chest level. Any lower and the neck bends too far, causing the voice to direct itself to the floor. Speak directly to your listeners.

Handling last-minute nerves

In Chapter One we looked at ways of preparing yourself for nerves prior to the big day. Immediately prior to or during your speech nerves may still strike, so here are some last-minute ways of dealing with them.

Get comfortable with the space: Don't add more pressure by arriving at the last moment. You'll feel calmer if you know where everything is, how it all works and from where you'll be speaking. If possible, arrive with sufficient time for a run-through, too.

Find a friendly face: Speakers are often intimidated by a new audience. However, audiences rarely want speakers to be boring or to do a bad job. They want you to succeed. Find a friendly or welcoming face in the audience, smile back at them and it will do you no end of good.

Tripping over your words? If you can't find the word, pause, and if it doesn't come to you, just use 'thing' if it's a noun, ask the audience to prompt you, or use a sentence to describe the word you can't find. If you mispronounce or trip over your words just say it again correctly or acknowledge it with a simple phrase such as: 'I could have said that a little better', and move on. The most important thing is to *look* unworried by your slip.

Shaking: If you get the shakes the audience will often be unaware of it unless you make it obvious. To avoid this:

- Grasp your hands comfortably together in front of you between your waist and chest, without fidgeting or moving them.

- Don't hold notes – they'll advertise your shakes; instead, use a podium or small prompt cards (see page 83).

- If you're using a mike, rest the hand holding the mike gently against your chest and this will steady it.

When you walk onto the platform...

Make a good first impression

If walking to a platform, adopt an easy gait. Arms swinging naturally, body straight.

Give your audience your best wishes from word one. Show them that you are happy to be there, by wearing a relaxed warm expression. It is easy to appear stern-faced when nervous. The facial muscles can get tight. Practising a few mouth, lip and tongue exercises beforehand can help. (See Chapter One.)

Animate your body movements

The audience needs a sense of direction, a feeling that the speaker is in charge and can be trusted. Positive body language can help achieve this.

If using a lectern, place your notes on it with a quick glance down, and then look at your audience. Remember to keep the eyes up as much as possible and certainly during the introduction, when you should be looking at the audience.

Smile as you speak

Smile as you make your opening remarks. This is a very difficult thing to do, but necessary. Thereafter use dimpling of the face. Imagine having a face lift! The cheeks and lips are slightly raised, as though you are about to smile. This way you appear more approachable and attractive.

Focus on your audience

When there is a large audience present, it is sometimes difficult to know where to look when making a speech. If there is strong stage lighting, it is unlikely that you will be able to see your audience, in which case individual eye contact is impossible. If there is a central exit light at the back of the hall, use that as your main focus point. In between times the eyes can travel to the right-hand side of the hall and then the left, always honing back to the exit sign. This gives the illusion of looking at your audience.

Jokes

Make sure any jokes in your speech are acceptable to the audience. Don't risk offending or embarrassing anyone. Refer to Chapter Eight for detailed advice on using jokes.

Accepting compliments

Some people find it hard to accept compliments. They feel uncomfortable, become self-effacing and embarrassed and dismiss, deny or overlook the giver's good opinion. These are negative and rejecting responses to compliments that have been given in good faith. Pleased to receive them, confident speakers will respond to plaudits by accepting them with grace and charm. If you are commended, return the compliment by accepting it. Retain eye contact with the giver and express your gratitude with warmth and sincerity. A simple 'Thank you' or 'Thank you, I appreciate that' can be sufficient.

SUMMARY: POINTS TO CHECK BEFORE THE SPEECH

Give yourself permission to feel nervous! Use feelings of nervousness to propel you into action. This will give you the energy needed to deliver a strong, animated speech.

Use relaxation and breathing exercises to keep nerves under control. Correct breathing will also support the voice.

Be gentle with yourself: Be generous with self-praise. Criticize yourself constructively.

Observe and listen: Learn your craft by listening to other good speakers and observing their style and delivery.

Keep the voice well oiled: Practise vocal exercises to improve quality, range and clarity.

Prepare well in advance. Try to look forward to the event. Imagine how you would feel if, after all your hard work, the speech was cancelled at the last minute.

Greet your audience with pleasure. Let them see that you are glad to be there.

Give yourself a 'facial': Practise facial exercises to tone the muscles and help you relax. Rehearse speaking in warm tones. Imagine giving a talk on the radio. Use a 'vocal smile' to express yourself.

Physical awareness: A relaxed bearing will help promote a feeling of well-being and will transmit to the audience an air of confidence. Release tension in the shoulders and neck by practising Exercises 2, 3, and 4 in Chapter One.

Irritating habits: Try asking a close friend to tell you what yours are – a test of real friendship!

Appearance: Wear clothes that are comfortable, but smart. Choose colours and styles that are flattering and provide some interest; for example, an arresting tie for the man, an unusual scarf for the woman.

Arrive in good time: If you have been able to liaise with the programme organizer you will know whether or not you can run through a few last-minute preparations such as checking for lighting and sound.

Be prepared: If this is a business presentation or a talk to a local society or group, will there be a 'Question Time' at the end of the evening?

speechmakers' bible

chapter 6

Business presentations and after-dinner speaking

'Make sure you have finished speaking before your
audience has finished listening.'
*Dorothy Sarnoff, 21st century American author
and orator*

When in a work environment we more normally refer to 'presentations' rather than 'speeches'. Speeches in a business context are normally reserved for someone leaving a job or role, or alternatively when attempting to motivate or inspire others. What is the difference between a speech and a presentation?

SPEECH	PRESENTATION
Little interaction	Much interaction
No or few visual aids	Visual aids normally used
Often larger audiences	May be just a few people
Normally to inspire, acknowledge or entertain	Aim to inform or persuade
Can be generic	Normally tailored to audience/customers

In other chapters you will find examples of speeches for you to draw on. Since a feature of the business speech is that it is normally unscripted to ensure a natural delivery, we focus instead in this chapter on the frameworks around which to structure effective business presentations. Scripted business presentations are likely to come across as unnatural, untailored and mechanical so we will look at ways to avoid this.

The effectiveness of a business presentation, no matter how large or small the audience, is largely dependent on the manner in which it is delivered. A pleasing tonality of voice, use of emphasis, pause, pace and volume can enhance a presentation and greatly increase audience interest, which may be of vital importance to those involved. To this end, it is imperative that you prepare yourself and your material well. Refer back to the previous chapters for help with planning your speech, improving your voice control, personal presentation and help with coping with nerves, and consider also the following.

PLANNING YOUR PRESENTATION

If you have been asked to make a business presentation, consider this checklist before you commence your planning:

- Who will be in the audience? Will they be all levels of employees, a small management team, or newcomers to the company?

- Is the occasion formal or informal? (This will affect the style of speech as well as the clothing you choose to wear.)

- Do the audience have any prior knowledge of the subject? (Refer back to Chapter Two for more advice about this.)

- How many speakers are there? If there are others, check with them what they plan to do on the day. (Refer to Chapter Five for advice about communicating with the organizers.)

- Will you be introduced or will you be introducing yourself? (Again, see Chapter Five for guidelines on this.)

- Will you be able to use visual aids? (There is advice on using visual aids on page 67.)

- Will there be a question and answer session at the end? (Refer to pages 162–9.)

- Will you be preparing sheets and handouts to accompany your presentation?

Preparation

All the advice given in the preparation and planning chapters of this book equally apply to business presentations and it is worth highlighting some of the areas where they need special tailoring or emphasis.

Presentation length

At an informal or non-work speech speakers are easily forgiven small overruns. In a business context, the 'window of opportunity' is frequently limited by busy working diaries and timetables; an hour means just that, an hour. An example of this may be when a person has only a one-hour slot to present their company and product to a customer. This makes accurate timing and pacing even more vital. See the tips in Chapter Two for how to get the duration spot on.

The audience

In Chapter Two there is a checklist to diagnose your audience type. In a business context you may need to consider the following additional information:

• How long have they been with the company?

• Which subsidiary/division are they in?

• What department are they in?

• What is their role/are their roles?

• How will my presentation subject affect them?

• What do they already know about my product/service?

• What is their opinion about my product/services

• How senior are they in the business?

• What are their names? (If it is a small audience.)

• What role do they play in the decision-making process?

Cultural and language sensitivity

The working world has undergone a huge and rapid process of globalization in the last 10 years as companies become more and more international. It is not uncommon to find companies in non-Anglophone countries adopting English as their working language. This means that presentations are now given around the world daily where none of the participants are native English speakers. The factors discussed in Chapter Two still hold true:

• Preparation: get a work colleague from the country you are presenting in to rehearse with and coach you.

• Speak at an appropriate pace and with pauses.

• To assist the audience's comprehension, use visual aids that reflect what you are saying.

• Keep your content and language simple, avoiding acronyms, abbreviations and complicated constructions.

Reliable and accurate reference material

In a non-work speech speakers will draw considerably upon anecdotes, quotes, stories and humour. With business presentations the goal of the presentation may require much more robust reference material to achieve an aim such as persuading a client in order to win a large piece of business. Therefore, business presenters are more likely to draw on some of the sources below than those mentioned earlier for the non-business speaker:

• **Facts:** These should be referenced and rock solid reliable. Typical facts could be features of your product or service such as dimensions or specifications.

- **Statistics:** These must be well sourced in order to be credible and convincing. Statistics figure highly in business presentations – for example, the marketing department may be describing the demographics of their target market or using market research to identify gaps in the market for new products: *'Nine out of ten owners said their pet preferred it.'*

- **Quotes and testimonials:** These are real favourites in advertising materials where companies use quotes from satisfied customers in an attempt to convince prospects. *'After using a leading competitor for the last 15 years, I used Glitz washing powder and made my clothes the whitest they've ever been.'*

- **Case studies:** When trying to attract new customers, businesses often need to talk 'war stories', detailing their past success for other companies.

Visual aids

When speechmaking outside the work environment the goal is often to acknowledge or entertain and so visual aids do not figure so greatly as in a business presentation – imagine an after-dinner speaker dimming the lights and projecting a set of Powerpoint slides, or the father of the bride bringing out a set of flip charts! In business presentations the focus is different, frequently concentrating on informing or persuading. To achieve both these goals it is necessary to present considerable reference material in a clear and compelling way. This is why visual aids are frequently vital to business presentations. See Chapter Two for guidance on their most effective use.

Structuring your presentation

Speeches are normally a lot more emotionally charged than business presentations. Their objective is to inspire, appeal, thank, celebrate or honour. To introduce too much structure to a speech would often be to break the moment or take away from the emotion and mood that the speechmaker has worked so hard to create.

However, structure is much more important in business presentations since, frequently, the objective is to persuade or inform and is (rightly or wrongly) more rational in nature. To achieve this goal it is important that the audience retain the main points made and are able to follow the exact line of argument, story or process. Effective use of structure is key to the process of understanding and being memorable.

In Chapter Two on planning and preparation we saw a standard format of structure:

- **Opening comments:** You can make these pretty thorough when you are giving a business presentation, as it is much more acceptable and normal to run through housekeeping and administration than it would be for a wedding or after-dinner speech!

- **Engagement item and Link:** It is vital that the engagement item be relevant and well linked in a business presentation, since in the modern world stressed-out executives have little time to listen to a drawn-out, only tenuously connected story from your schooldays. Sensitivity around jokes is even more important in a work setting than outside. An inappropriate joke could get you fired, so stick to the golden rule: if you're not sure, don't use it.

- **Subject and agenda:** Agenda points set up the audience for what is coming and ensure what they need to hear will be covered.

- **Content:** Must be clear, relevant, pitched at the right level and, if necessary, persuasive. The content should be sub-divided into your three or four Agenda points or key messages:

    Agenda Point 1

    Agenda Point 2

    Agenda Point 3

- **Summary:** The summary is important to ensure retention of your key messages and that you don't just stop dead.

- **Conclusion:** In business it is important to have action-orientated meetings and for people to be clear on what the next steps are.

Here are some outlines for a variety of business presentations:

Fundraising speech
Situation/need
Analysis
Appeal and how to contribute

Strategy presentation
Short term
Medium term
Long term

Sales conferences
Budget
Actual sales
Variances

Prizegiving/awards
Describe category
The contenders/nominees
The winner

Openings: Building/fair
Welcomes
Acknowledgements and thanks
Declaration and naming

State of the industry
Past
Present
Future

Disclosure speech

Background situation

Results

Next steps and actions

Remedies

Choices

Analysis

Selection

Product presentation

Customer need

Feature of the product

Benefits to the customer

Issue solving

Problem

Choices

Solution

Linking elements of structure

When using a structure, business presenters are often guilty of jumping without warning between the different sections of their presentations. This catches the audience out and should be avoided by the use of smooth links between one part and the next. The effective use of links will allow your audience to follow more easily your line of thought or story and prepare them for what they are about to hear. In the box below you'll find a collection of useful linking phrases:

LINKING PHRASES

I'm going to cover three main aspects...

I'm going to discuss three different points of view...

Let's keep four key elements in mind...

Let's turn to...

Initially, let's look at...

To begin with...

To start with, we have...

Moving to our next agenda item...

Next, I'll come to...

On the other hand...

Now we'll examine...

To continue this line of thought, we have...

Our next important element is...

Which brings me to...

Which leads me to...

With this point in mind...

I would like to discuss...

We recommend...

And in keeping with this...

In response to that...

This will serve to introduce our subject...

Finally, we come to...

Lastly, we have...

Finally, then, let's look at...

Lastly, we have...

So much for...

That covers...

So, we've seen that...

And finally...

To resume...

Overall, we see...

So, let's now take an overview...

We have seen that...

Therefore...

Consequently...

To conclude...

A final thought to leave with you...

What I want you to take away from this...

I strongly recommend...

I strongly urge...

Clearly, our next step is...

Hooking your audience

Audience interest will be at its height at the beginning of a speech. After that there is a tendency for concentration to flag, with occasional periods of increased interest. If the audience senses the end of a talk, it will revive itself, anxious not to miss any vital information. The renewed interest is not, however, as strong as the initial curiousity.

From this we may deduce that:

• A strong introduction is important.

• An energetic introduction is important.

• Audiences desire strong direction.

So:

- State clearly the title of the presentation; e.g. 'Our topic is 'Industry today'.'

- State clearly the headlines under which you will speak: 'I will deal with this topic under five main headings.'

The listeners will have been led and motivated into a more attentive frame of mind by a speaker who is specific and aware of the needs of the audience.

Breaking up the presentation

If the presentation is quite a long one, let your listeners know when you have reached the end of the first part of the talk. This guides them and revives their interest. At least one conclusion will be necessary. Draw all the links of your chain together and sum up the points that you have already made. As a speaker, you should keep bringing the audience back to your attention. Listeners need to receive small mental shocks from time to time, otherwise the whole thing can be woolly and vague in their memories.

Feedback

End by summarizing. Reiteration is important if the audience is to retain what has been said. The more technical the presentation, the greater the need for clarity.

Taking the chair

An effective chairperson is rather like a good parent. He or she casts a caring eye over their charge without interfering on all fronts. They allow events to develop democratically, without denying the right of self-expression and freedom. They are firm without being authoritarian and crushing in their role, and they see that there is fair play.

If you consider becoming a chairperson, ask yourself these questions:

• Have I got leadership skills?

• How do I function in a group setting?

• Am I patient?

• Am I assertive?

• Do I possess a sense of fair play?

• Am I methodical?

You will have some idea what your communication skills are like from past records at school and college, or at work. Of course, we don't always see ourselves as others view us, but we often have a pretty good idea. If you are unsure as to whether or not you are suited for the job, pluck up courage and ask one or two good friends how you come across and encourage them to suggest areas where they think you could improve. For example, you may be assertive in some areas, but impatient or short-tempered in others. There are times when we may justify certain traits within ourselves, without stopping to re-evaluate our viewpoint. While you may not have taken a front-line position in the past, consider accepting an offer to take the chair.

The principal duties of the chairperson are to keep order, to deal with relevant business, to say who shall speak, and to put resolutions to the vote. The chairperson declares the opening and closing of meetings and is the general overseer of the proceedings. If there are speakers, they should always address the chairperson first before commencing their speech, often as Mr Chairman or Madam Chairwoman.

The chairperson will follow an agenda. This may include: a welcome and reasons for the meeting; apologies for absence; the minutes of the last meeting (which will have been taken down by the secretary); matters arising from the last meeting; reports (such as a treasurer's report); points that may arise from these reports; any other business; the date set for the next meeting.

Introducing a speaker

If you are introducing a speaker, do it with momentum. Here are some suggestions:

- Say his or her name strongly, clearly and slowly. This gives the audience time to digest the information.

- Introduce the person with enthusiasm and warmth.

- Include him or her in your body language. Look at the person briefly and turn yourself in their direction at least once. Practise swivelling your body round, using the feet as a pivot.

- 'Ladies and gentlemen, John Smith.' As you speak include an arm gesture at this point. Small movements look awkward and will not be seen at the back. Use a wide gesture and let it flow from the waist. Practise until this comes naturally.

Make sure that your voice does not drop when your body is turned away from the audience.

Thanking the speaker

If you make the introduction, it is important that you listen carefully to everything the speaker has to say. You can then include in your vote of thanks several points of interest that may have been made during the speech.

Avoid a eulogistic vote of thanks. This can be embarrassing for the speaker, and may not be in accordance with the views of the audience.

If the speech was poor, a polite but short vote of thanks will suffice. This avoids embarrassment all round, as the speaker may know his or her performance was weak, and any hypocrisy will most likely be detected.

Your vote of thanks can be formal or informal.

SUMMARY OF A CHAIRPERSON'S DUTIES

As a chairperson, you will lead events, so remember:

• Learn all the rules and procedures before starting. Ensure that you are told about relevant issues that need addressing. The secretary deals with the minutes, but you should look at these before the meeting.

• Arrive in good time to make any preparations.

• Be firm but friendly.

• Keep to the agenda and be succinct. Avoid straying from the point. Use interim summaries to help you and to guide members.

• Deal kindly and encouragingly with those people who are shy at speaking out. Sometimes they can contribute most.

• Aim to foster a wide spread of opinions. Some people love to talk for talking's sake, and meetings can provide the perfect opportunity for this to happen. Be polite but firm. Suggest to them that someone else might like to express their view. If no-one is forthcoming, continue to the next piece of business.

• Be aware of the needs of those present. Meetings can be very protracted and boring, so keep up the pace but avoid rushing. Be firm, and guided by what is going on around you. Maintain good eye contact with those present.

- As a chairperson, you may also be expected to host visiting speakers. Ensure that they are made to feel comfortable. You may have liaised with them before their arrival.

- Ensure that the seating and microphones are arranged correctly and are suitable for the speaker's needs. If it is possible, give them time to acclimatize themselves to the setting in which they will speak.

- Ensure that you know the speaker's names and that the pronunciation is correct, so that when you introduce them to the audience, you get it right.

- You may know the length of the speech or speeches in advance, but it is a good idea to double-check, particularly if there are several talks taking place. This can pre-empt any future embarrassment should a speaker over-run.

- If a speech does over-run or is exceptionally tedious, you can scribble a note signalling the speaker to wind up as soon as possible. You are justified in doing so, if you have indicated the time limit in advance.

- At question time following a speech, questions may either go through you, or be directly addressed to the speaker. If there is aggravation caused by an audience member, intervene but avoid unnecessary nannying. (See also pages 167–70.)

- Remember to send a letter of thanks to a visiting speaker, and to include travelling expenses, if required.

Handling large audiences

Speaking to large audiences involves exactly the same principles employed with small audiences. The main difference is how the speaker *feels*. In everyday life we frequently find ourselves speaking to smaller 'audiences' such as at meetings or when addressing our family or a group of friends. Consequently, we feel more at ease presenting to smaller audiences.

When faced with a large number of people staring at us, a different dynamic occurs. During the course of a normal conversation one-to-one, our interlocutor will be looking at us for perhaps 50–60% of the time when talking and a little more when they are listening. However, imagine what it would feel like if you noticed a person staring at you without looking away at all. Most people would find this intimidating and would feel distinctly uncomfortable. When faced with larger audiences, there will always be a large number of people looking at you, wherever you look. This arouses primeval feelings of fear, probably as we associate the situation with one of being faced with a large number of potentially dangerous rivals.

This fear in turn causes the speaker to do one of three things: they will bury themselves in their notes, find refuge in their visual aids, or fix on a point on the back wall behind their audience. The key aim for speakers with larger audiences is to gain comfort, or at least give the impression of comfort by engaging the audience with eye contact. This is easier said than done and a technique is needed. This technique is known as 'grouping'.

When grouping, the speaker chooses a number of individual audience members spread throughout the room and lets their eyes rest on each individual for a few seconds before moving to the next person. This makes the people in the vicinity of the 'target' think the speaker is addressing and looking at them. Next time you watch *Question Time* on television, notice how, when the audience is being asked for questions from the floor, a group of individuals around the 'target' all think that the chairperson is pointing at them.

Beyond grouping, most other principles remain the same as for any public speaking. The following should be remembered as special considerations to get right:

Make sure visual aids can be read: Large audiences normally mean that those at the back will be further away. Check they can see.

Make sure you can be heard: If you don't have a microphone take care to project. Get a helper to stand at the back of the room whilst you practise, and trim the volume appropriately.

Ensure you aren't blinkered: There is a temptation to focus mainly on those in the centre of a large audience. Make sure you include the 'wings' of your audience or even those behind you if you are set up centrally.

Smile and be yourself: Remember, there is no difference in *how* you address large compared to small audiences; it's only how you *feel*, so give the audience the impression that you feel confident and in control.

Taking questions

In Chapter Two we looked at planning and preparation for questions, which is crucial for a smooth-running session. Now, we'll look at how you handle the questions. Don't see every question an attack on you or your presentation. It is possible that the audience are asking the question because you haven't explained something very well. So what are the stages to go through to handle questions?

Listen: Look at the person posing the question and don't interrupt, even if you're sure you know what the question is going to be. Interrupting will create a negative emotional response on the part of the person asking the question. If it is a particularly large audience and you have a mike on remember to repeat the question so that the remainder of the audience are able to hear what was asked.

Check: Make sure you have understood what is being asked. If you are not sure what issue is being raised ask the questioner to clarify, perhaps by rephrasing the question or alternatively by asking them to give an example of what they mean.

Reword: You may reword their question in order to ensure that you have correctly interpreted their meaning. This is often positioned with introductory phrases such as: 'If I've understood you correctly, you want to know...' If it is perfectly obvious what they mean, do not attempt to check or reword; they may think you are being patronizing or think you're just stalling for time before answering.

Choose: Once you have understood the question, take a brief moment to choose how you are going to respond to it. Sometimes it is necessary to choose between an answer and a response. An answer is the straightforward, rational reply; a response, however, is the reply you choose to give – it may be direct or can be a diversionary statement or message on another issue. Politicians are masters of employing responses to questions as an alternative to giving answers that may put them in a difficult position. If asked a question that you know will be answered later on you may have to choose your response. The general rule is that if it is quick and easy to give the answer on the spot and won't interrupt your flow or story then answer it. It can be frustrating for an audience to be told to wait when a quick question is asked, without being given a reason to do so beyond: 'We'll be coming to that later.' However, if there is a good reason to do so, you may defer a question provided you ask permission and give a good reason for waiting. For example: 'Thank you for your question, we'll actually be coming onto that subject later and it will make more sense within the overall context if I answer it at that stage. Would that be OK? Great, just remind me if I don't cover it when we come to that section. Thanks.'

Respond: If you decide to reply, you should then answer the question looking at the person who posed the question and 'grouping' the audience if the answer runs to some length. If relevant, consider including examples in your answer, as they often bring concepts to life.

Verify: After you have answered the question, go back to the person who posed it and check that it actually hit the nail on the head. For example: 'Did that answer your question?'

TOP TIPS FOR HANDLING QUESTIONS

Don't know the answer? If you don't know the answer to a question, be honest and tell the audience you don't know. There are a number of good reasons for doing so:

• You will be perceived as honest and it lends credibility to all the other assertions you make and answers you give.

• It is a great rapport builder with audiences, since we have all been asked questions we don't know the answer to and so feel for someone in the same situation. You will be seen as someone 'just like me' from the audience's perspective.

• Audiences can read people like a book. If you start bluffing, everything about your manner and verbal and nonverbal communication will give this away.

• If you get it wrong you are likely to be exposed, either after the session or, even worse, as you answer during the session.

• Reply simply to the questioner, stating: 'I don't have the answer to that question and what I'll do is find out and give you a call by Friday with the answer.' Stating 'I'll get back to you' is not sufficiently reassuring or action orientated. To gain the confidence of your audience, always state by when and how and then, of course, follow up on it.

Take the pressure off you and put it back on the audience: When being asked questions, a good tactic with a smaller audience is to 'bounce' the question and throw it back to the audience for someone else to answer or to give their viewpoint on. This means the tension is reflected away from you. Always ensure you tie up the answer at the end and verify with the questioner that the response did cover the question. Do not use this tactic just because you don't know the answer unless you preface your phrase with: 'I'm not sure on that one – does anyone know the answer?'

Take an expert: If you are presenting particularly technical material or content that you are not familiar with, it is often useful to take an expert along. Even if they don't speak during the main presentation they are often invaluable during questions. Again, this shifts more tension away from you as a presenter.

Don't get personal: Even if it seems as though the question is an insult or attack, keep your head. We look at dealing with hecklers below.

Consider 'planted' questions: If you fear that there may be some reticence in the audience to ask the first question, you can consider planting someone to get things going. Be careful that this question is not too crude, obvious or emotionally/politically loaded or else your intent may be undermined.

Conference panel speaking and handling questions as a team

When speaking at a conference as a member of a panel or at any team business presentation the great work you have done in preparation and delivery of the main body of your speech can be easily undone if you don't appear to be a well-drilled team during your question and answer session.

The first thing to establish is whether you will have a team 'lead' or facilitator. If you choose to have a team lead, this person will ask for and redirect the question to the appropriate team member to answer, unless they are the one best placed to do so. By having the lead as a conduit for the questions, the group can appear well orchestrated and also gain an extra few valuable moments to consider their answer.

One major way that teams appear disunified during questions is when several different people add to an answer that someone else has just given – sometimes disagreeing with it, sometimes confusing it. The overall impression it creates is that the person adding to the answer does not think their teammate has been sufficiently competent in answering the question. As a general guideline, teams should agree that a maximum of one or, in extremis, two people should be permitted to add to the answer of another. Occasionally, audience members may pose their question to the 'wrong' panel member, i.e. a person who is not the expert in the subject of the question being asked. The team should agree before the session what to do in this eventuality.

Normally this will mean that the person asked will thank the audience member and then suggest that their colleague would be better placed to answer the question.

It may help to use a simple table like the one below to agree beforehand who will tackle which questions. This prevents people from talking over each other or fighting for air time.

Question subject area	Who primes?	Key 'adder'
Marketing	Marketing & Sales Director	CEO
Sales	Marketing & Sales Director	Sales Manager
Production	Manufacturing Director	Operations Director
Strategy	CEO	Chairman

Dealing with hecklers/difficult people

Speeches and presentations are rather unusual in a communication context in that they tend to be verbally one-way, with the exception of question and answer sessions. This rather unbalanced relationship forces certain audience members to break the unwritten 'rule' of obedient silence and start heckling or otherwise being difficult. So what are some of the ways of handling hecklers?

Don't be seen to be reacting: When heckled, it's important that you continue giving an impression of confidence, calm and control. If the heckler was funny why not join in the laughter? It could well help in building rapport with your audience.

Divide and conquer: If you are faced with a persistent troublemaker who is continuing to raise issues not relevant to your agenda, suggest that the subject is out of scope, but you'd be happy to deal with it in a one-to-one discussion afterwards. As hecklers are often driven by ego and playing to the audience, the issue mysteriously disappears afterwards.

Depersonalizing issues: When an issue is being discussed it can appear to be adversarial between the speaker and the questioner, especially if first-person statements are used, such as: '*I* think we should move on.' This is likely to set up a battle of wills. A way of depersonalizing the issue and moving tension off you is to let those around you deal with the heckler. For example, bring in the rest of the group with statements such as: 'Perhaps the remainder of the audience would like to move on to ensure we don't run out of time?' Invariably, audiences feel as irritated as you do by most troublemakers. Do, however, make sure that you have correctly read the audience's likely reaction, otherwise you could find yourself in an embarrassing situation!

Defusing: One of the core skills of a communicator is the ability to be able to see an argument or discussion from the other person's point of view. It is particularly useful for defusing an emotional heckler. It is extremely disarming to a heckler if you acknowledge their point of view, without necessarily conceding that you agree with it. Arguing aggressively tends to have the effect of throwing oil on the fire. Statements such as: 'I can certainly understand that point of view' help build bridges as long as you don't follow it up with a killer 'but'.

Interruptions

Hecklers are for the most part fairly innocent, but you may be faced with more concerted interrupters whose sole aim is to undermine or disrupt your speech or presentation. In this case the methods above may not be enough. Other tactics include:

- Looking to the chairperson for an intervention.

- Indicating that the heckler will have their opportunity later to ask questions.

- Stopping speaking until they have burnt themselves out.

- Asking the heavies from security to eject them!

However, not all interruptions are malign so don't always take disruptions as deliberate. These could include:

Loo: When you've got to go, you've got to go. If one or two people walk out to answer the call of nature simply carry on as if nothing has happened. If increasing numbers seem to be making their way to the exit it could be because you've been going on for too long; consider whether you need to give people a break.

Mobile phones. During your introduction, ask people to switch off their mobile phones. If you are in a small presentation and a phone goes off and its owner doesn't leave, stop presenting until they've finished their call. After the interruption, remind the audience again that the remainder of the audience would appreciate it if they switched their phones off. Remember to ask that *all* electronic devices be switched off, as machines that send and receive e-mails are becoming increasingly common.

Standing to avoid falling asleep: Sometimes people stand to the side or at the back of the room to avoid falling asleep. These people are at least showing good intent so don't draw attention to them (they may have young children who have kept them awake all night). If a few people start doing this, it could mean that, as above, you might have been talking for too long without taking a break. On the other hand, it may be that your delivery is not sufficiently dynamic and you need to raise your game. This can be done by any of the following:

- Increasing the modulation of your voice in terms of volume, projection, and variety of tone or pace.

- Using audience participation by giving them something to do, getting them physically involved by making them stand up, or getting them involved looking at something.

- Using a question and answer session to get them more involved or on their toes.

- Introducing visual aids such as videos to recapture their attention.

How did you do?

Consider these points when assessing your speech or listening to others. You will inevitably be asked to speak again, and in business, it is best to use every opportunity for improvement. The plus points are on the left, minuses on the right.

Personality

Confident	Uncertain
Authoritative	Unsure
Composed	Edgy
Lively	Dull
Good audience contact	Withdrawn
Good audience reaction	Failure to move audience
Good eye contact	Eyes directed away from audience
Fluent speech	Abrupt/disjointed
Appropriate humour	Unimaginative/boring in content
Appropriate gestures	Distracting/unnecessary gestures
Relaxed movement	Over-tense

Voice and speech

Clear enunciation	Unclear enunciation
Efficient breath control	Poor breath control
Adequate voice projection	Weak voice projection or over-loud
Variety of tone using pause, pace, power, pitch	Monotonous delivery

The introduction

Imaginative	Mundane

The development of the speech

Logical	Muddled
Economical	Disjointed/rambling
Clear stages of progression	Too protracted
Accuracy of facts	Inaccuracy of facts
Efficient use of language	Pedantic/difficult to understand/long-winded
Use of humour	Humourless

Keeping to time limit	Over-long
Appropriate use of emphasis to aid clarity	Lack of definition
Stages recapped and checked; use of interim as well as final summary	Insensitive to audience needs
Keeping to the point	Digressing
Aim and scope of speech given	Lack of direction/vague/ poor format

Informal speeches

Informal speeches require subtle changes from their more formal cousins. There is more of a peer relationship between the speaker and audience with less rigidity, more interaction and more of a free-flowing agenda. How does this manifest itself in the speech?

Structure: Rather than a formal set structure, speakers will allow a more loose discussion. The 'tell 'em' method is very useful for informal structure to help highlight key messages.

Content: In terms of the actual language used, speakers should remain conscious of the trap of becoming too formal in their use of language when there may be a more simple and direct way of saying something. A conversational style with everyday language is more likely to ensure the appropriate informal tone is set.

Your clothes: Even small actions like taking off a suit jacket, rolling up your sleeves or wearing slightly less formal clothing can help impart a more relaxed atmosphere to a speech.

Use of voice: When talking informally the speaker needs to make sure they are not using too much power in their voice, either by employing too much volume or over-projecting beyond the furthest member of the audience. Using too much power may convey too much authority or too much of a 'tell' attitude, which could potentially alienate the audience and make them less likely to contribute or ask questions.

Use of visual aids and presenting props: If the speaker wishes to set an informal tone the use of aids should be minimized. This is particularly true of the use of a podium or similar, which it is easy to interpret as a barrier or shield between the speaker and the audience, thus creating an artificially formal atmosphere. The same is true for visual aids. Can you imagine someone using a set of visual aids during a speech at a wedding or funeral? Absolutely not. Similarly, at work the use of highly prepared visual aids would not be reflective of an informal, open and two-way relationship where each person's input is equally valued.

Scripting: Throughout this chapter we have encouraged you to avoid scripted speeches for the majority of business presentations. This is particularly true of informal presentations. The audience is less likely to be relaxed if their speaker is following a script; they will see little opportunity to ask questions and may feel there is too much of a concealed or structured intent behind the words.

Movement around the presenting room: If the presenter remains standing directly in front of their seated audience the mood created tends to be formal. This is because we relate it closely to the teacher–pupil relationship that we experienced at school. This can be useful when we need to maintain or exert control over our audience, when we need to impart, teach or train information, principally in one 'tell' direction, or when we need to maintain eye contact with a larger group of people. However, we can create a more informal mood by moving around the room; for example:

Moving from position to position in front of the audience: The amount of formality can be reduced slightly if the speaker moves at certain moments of the presentation to create different angles between him or her and the audience. This is done by moving consciously from one point to another and can assist in signposting different parts of the presentation. It also has the effect of ensuring that the speaker is not always stood head-on to the audience, which could be perceived as the most aggressive positioning.

Sitting: By sitting, the speaker immediately puts him or herself more on the level of the audience. In this way he or she may create a more equal relationship of peers where each person's opinion has the same value. The downside of presenting seated is that the speaker may lose some control, and engaging with all the audience members by eye contact becomes more difficult.

Sitting amongst the audience: By sitting amongst the audience, the speaker can take this one step further by embedding him or herself with the audience. This makes the speaker seem even more a member of the same team, rather than the us-and-them or confrontational attitude that may be apparent when he or she presents standing straight-on and in front of the audience.

Walking amongst the audience: By walking amongst the audience, the speaker reduces the distance and is able to move into positions where he or she can engage more directly and closely with all the people. It is representative of a more dynamic style and can allow the speaker to approach any particular people he or she is talking about. When doing this, speakers need to be careful not to stop for too long behind any one person, since it is likely to make those audience members feel threatened or singled out in the same way as a teacher may stand behind the naughty schoolboy in class.

Greetings, thanks and retirement speeches

Many informal work speeches are not directly linked with the actual execution of the business of the company, but are related to welcoming new employees or people who have transferred in, thanking those who have performed a particularly good job, or saying goodbye to those leaving the business. Here are some simple guidelines for this type of occasion:

Be structured and concise: We have all been subjected to over-lengthy speeches that consist of a rambling and endless list of thank yous. Instead, employ one of the structures you'll find in Chapter Two. Work out what the principal areas you want to talk about are. Say it once and say it well, then sit down. As ever, rehearsal will help make sure that you aren't going to bang on for too long.

Avoid scripting: Greetings, thanks and retirement speeches have one thing in common: they should contain an appropriate degree of emotion. Only the most gifted public speakers are able to appear sincere when reading from a script or delivering a memorized speech, so, as described elsewhere, it is better to have prompts of the different areas you will talk about and then find the words naturally at the time. In this way the speaker is far more likely to appear to be sincere when welcoming, thanking or praising.

Proximity and attention: We tend to move closer to the things and people we like or appreciate – for example, our friends, partners and family, or in admiring a particular piece of sculpture, when a 'please do not touch' sign may be necessary to keep our hands off. In the same way, when greeting, thanking or praising, the speaker should consider moving closer to the subject being talked about. These speeches are not about the speaker's ability to entertain, but to articulate the feelings and sentiments of the speaker and the rest of the audience towards the subject of the speech. By moving closer to, or standing next to them it ensures that the well-deserved attention is where it should be.

Work parties and after-dinner speeches

Work-related parties

The office Christmas party will, of course, be a very relaxed affair and any speech given here should usually be humorous (without giving offence) and remain up-beat and congratulatory, thanking everyone for their commitment and contributions over the previous year. Any other personnel matters will include birthdays (see Chapter Seven for more information about such celebrations), retirement, leaving parties and promotions. As a general rule, keep comments positive and light-hearted, but well-intentioned and well-researched.

After-dinner speaking

A person is invited to give an after-dinner speech because he or she is either well known in a particular field, of high repute, or renowned for after-dinner speaking. To receive such an invitation is an honour that should not be taken lightly.

Take care in the preparation of your speech and make absolutely certain that it runs for the time required, is relevant and entertaining. As a rule, an after-dinner speech is longer than other speeches. But the basic rules of preparation and delivery covered in the earlier chapters still prevail. If you are in doubt, refer back to them.

If you are likely to be called upon as a regular after-dinner speaker, or if you decide to take it up professionally, keep a fund of anecdotes relative to your subject. If these relate to your own personal experiences so much the better. Refer to Chapter Eight for material to entertain your audience with.

CHECKLIST FOR INFORMAL OR AFTER-DINNER SPEECHES:

Make sure the audience is prepared so that they know to take a loo break if they need one prior to the speech.

Attract attention by striking the table or a glass, then wait for sufficient quiet before beginning.

Don't expect complete silence, there will always be a degree of background noise.

Use an appropriate engagement item (see Chapter Two). This a social occasion so you will have to work harder than usual with a strong engagement item to gain their attention.

If you were a professional after-dinner speaker you would be expected to sing for your supper with a speech of appropriate length to warrant your fee. At business dinners, however, you will be better served by being to the point. If people take bets on how long you will speak for, it is going on for too long.

When speaking, try to use personal stories and anecdotes. As discussed elsewhere in the book, they are far more interesting to listen to than a dry script.

Ensure you engage with all the tables at the dinner. If necessary by turning around at certain points or moving around the room (see above).

Toasts

If you are making a toast at the end of your speech, remember it consists of two parts, asking people to stand, then proposing the toast. These should remain separate to avoid awkward confusion and muddle.

1. Standing: Firstly, get everyone on their feet with an appropriate phrase such as: 'Ladies and Gentleman, please stand and join me in a toast', and then patiently wait until all are standing. This also allows time for people to charge their glasses if necessary.

2. Toasting: When all are standing with charged glasses, complete the toast.

SUMMARY: FINAL CHECKLIST

After you have prepared the presentation, check it using these questions:

• Who is my audience?

• What is their level of understanding of the subject?

• Am I pitching my messages at that level?

• What would they like to get out of my presentation?

• What is my goal for them?

• Does my presentation have a beginning, a middle and an end?

• Have I made my opening and closing particularly compelling and interesting?

• Are my messages clear?

• Have I removed any jargon, acronyms and abbreviations the audience will not understand?

• Is my reference data accurate, reliable and well-sourced?

• Have I rehearsed with someone who has given me impartial feedback?

- Have I allowed sufficient time for questions? (At least 25%.)

- Have I checked the room? Will everyone be able to see and hear what is going on?

- On the day, how and when will I be able to gain access to the room?

- Do I know how the audiovisual equipment works?

- What will I do if the audiovisual equipment fails?

- Do I have a back-up copy of any visual aids that I will be using?

- Have I limited myself to one idea per visual aid?

- Have I focused on the message I'm trying to get over rather than on the data or visual aids?

- Have I practised how I will link each different section of my presentation?

- Have I included relevant examples, stories and anecdotes to bring the presentation to life?

- Have I eliminated any distractions about me – my clothes and appearance?

- Have I planned my opening comments to remove any distractions from the environment? External noise, asking for phones to be switched off, etc.

- Have I planned to arrive in good time? (One hour should be considered a benchmark amount of time for you to be able to make yourself at home, check audiovisuals, check room layout and have a final read through or rehearsal of your presentation.)

- What questions will I be asked?

- Are there likely to be major objections from the audience to my point of view? If so, what are they and how will I tackle them?

- How and when will I be getting feedback from the audience about the effectiveness of my presentation and the next steps from it?

- If you are presenting with others, have you had joint rehearsals so you know how you will interact?

- Look at each visual aid you have and ask yourself, so what? Or, why am I showing this slide? If you can't answer the question simply take it out.

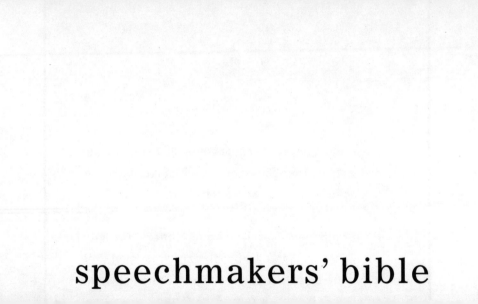

speechmakers' bible

chapter 7

Weddings and other family celebrations

Making a speech at a social occasion is often thought to be worse than having to stand up and speak at a business function. Not being able to enjoy the occasion for fear of embarrasing yourself in front of family and friends, is many peoples' worst nightmare. But whatever the celebration, be it a wedding, birthday, anniversary or funeral, you may be asked to make a speech. Don't panic. This chapter contains samples of speeches for every occasion.

Why make a speech? To express thanks, give information and, quite simply, because it is a tradition. And you also have a unique opportunity to pay public compliments to those you love most.

However, as with any speechmaking, and as repeated elsewhere in this book, there are certain things to avoid:

- Don't allow yourself to be overwhelmed by the concept of 'making a speech'. Instead, think of it rather as welcoming supportive, friendly people to the event and entertaining them for a few minutes – a sort of extended conversation that just happens to be with a larger than usual group of people.

- Don't leave things to the last minute, and unless you have a special gift for excellent and improvised public speaking, make sure you prepare what you are going to say well in advance.

- Don't underestimate your audience or, indeed, overestimate them – in age, experience, tolerance and understanding of your language or humour. Not everyone will be as familiar with the family history as you. There may be grannies and children present, so if using humour, keep it in proportion.

- Don't look down when you talk, don't whisper and don't shout, don't swear too much and don't improvise unless you feel really confident.

- Don't make your speech a series of loosely connected quotations from famous or other people. If you have written your own poem, don't perform it unless it has been read and vetted first.

- Don't forget that this speech is about the occasion and your relationship to the person/people involved. It is not a speech about you. It is not a vehicle for self-promotion or an audition for a reality show. Don't confuse 'eye contact' with 'I contact'.

Weddings

What is a speech and what is a toast? You can have a speech without a toast, and a toast without a speech, but at a wedding it is usual to combine the two.

Traditionally, the first speech, usually given by the bride's father or an old family friend, ends with the proposal of a toast to the health of the bride and bridegroom. The second speech is given as a reply to the first by the bridegroom and is concluded with the proposal of a toast to the bridesmaids. The best man then replies on behalf of the bridesmaids, and will conclude his speech by proposing a toast to the parents of the bride and bridegroom. And remember, women are increasingly being asked to take on the role of 'best man', so there is no need to feel awkward or unusual! So, throughout, read 'best man' to mean best man or woman.

The modern wedding, however, is flexible and the bride may feel comfortable making the speech on behalf of herself and her new husband, for example. Or the job of replying to the toast of the bridesmaids could be taken on by the chief bridesmaid rather than the best man. The bride may be given away by her mother, who can also speak if she so wishes.

Etiquette

The purpose of etiquette is to provide an easy set of rules that we can follow when we are in a hurry and want to make sure that we do not give offence to anybody. For example, we would not wish to neglect to thank the hosts, or fail to recognize the presence and importance of an honoured guest. The rules are most useful on formal occasions like weddings, and particularly when they happen only once in a lifetime. But because lifestyles are changing constantly the rules of etiquette are changing, too – a little slower than lifestyles perhaps, but still changing.

The timing of the speech

Circumstances vary in different countries and the rules of speechmaking differ for different religions. When speeches are made after seated dinners at lengthy, formal wedding receptions, they begin after all eating at the formal meal has finished, and are preceded by the announcement from the toastmaster: 'Ladies and Gentlemen, you may now smoke.' If the meal finishes with tea or coffee and wedding cake, speeches will be made after the cutting of the cake. There is a natural tendency to call for speeches after the bride and bridegroom have stood behind the cake to be photographed. It is easier to hold the attention of the diners at the end of the meal while they are seated and still too full to want to get up and start dancing.

However, if the celebration is to continue all evening and the tea or coffee and wedding cake are to be served later, it is possible to delay the cutting of the cake until after the speeches that conclude the meal. Whatever the wedding organizers decide, it is important to let the toastmaster and the speechmakers know, so that they are prepared and do not disappear at the vital moment.

Let us suppose you have late guests arriving after the wedding meal. What do you do? At seated dinners the number of guests invited to the meal may be limited by the cost or the size of the hall. Sometimes the seated guests are just the closest family and friends, while other friends, children, neighbours and work colleagues are invited for the dancing and party later in the day. A few guests who are invited to a midweek ceremony may not be able to leave work early, are delayed by rush hour traffic, or have to return home to change their clothes, and therefore they reach the reception after it has started.

Guests should not enter during the speeches, distracting the audience and disconcerting the speakers. But it is also necessary to avoid keeping them standing outside in the rain, or waiting in draughty corridors feeling unwanted while the meal finishes or the speeches are in progress. The hotel or hall staff can arrange chairs, drinks, and someone to direct and greet the late arrivals, who can then view the wedding presents, or be introduced to each other until a suitable moment arrives for them to enter the dining hall. They should then not be left standing if the other guests are seated, but shown to chairs on one side of the hall, or be directed to the seating plans so that they can fill the places kept for them, or go to seats left empty by 'no-shows' such as anyone taken ill at the last minute. You may wish to time the cake cutting and speeches so that later arrivals can enjoy them. The printed invitation can make any such timing clear.

What to do at buffets and informal weddings

At a buffet you ensure that elderly and infirm guests, and those who have travelled long distances, have seats near the buffet table so that they are not obliged to stand for a long period. If there is no toastmaster, the best man calls the attention of the guests to the start of the cake-cutting ceremony. The bride and bridegroom pose for photographs to be taken by the official photographer and guests who have brought their cameras. The chief bridesmaid, if she is not making a speech, can then lead the call for a speech.

The toastmaster

The first question you need to ask yourself is: do you need a toastmaster? At a large wedding it is usual to have a toastmaster to announce guests on the receiving line. He will know the traditional way to announce titles, that Mr and Mrs John Smith are husband and wife, Mrs John Smith is without her husband John who is away on business, Mrs Anne Smith is a widow, or that Mr John Smith and Mrs Anne Smith are the elderly aunt and uncle, brother and sister, not married to each other. The toastmaster opens the proceedings and keeps them flowing smoothly. In his absence the task would fall to the best man.

There are other benefits from employing a toastmaster. Since one essential quality of a good toastmaster is a loud voice (which often goes with an imposing, extrovert personality), they will get attention faster than you can (an alternative way to get the attention of the audience is to ask the band, if you have one, to do a drum roll for you). However, to ensure that proceedings go as you would wish, give the toastmaster instructions in advance, rather than piecemeal later.

If a toastmaster attends, he will begin his duties by announcing the names of the guests stepping forward to shake hands with the bridal party on the receiving line. Afterwards he will raise his voice and holler loud enough to be heard by the whole roomful of guests milling around chatting, perhaps talking excitedly with drinks in their hands: 'LADIES and GENTLEMEN! Pray be seated. DINNER is now being served!' When everyone has found their places he stands by the microphone at the top table, hammers on the table with a gavel and announces loudly: 'Ladies and Gentlemen, Pray SILENCE for the Reverend John Smith, who will now say grace.'

If there is no toastmaster, the best man may introduce the minister more simply: 'Ladies and Gentlemen, Reverend John Smith will now say grace.' The best man should check in advance the correct title and form of address for the minister, Archbishop, Chief Rabbi, or whoever will be attending. Is it Reverend, the Reverend, Mr, Mrs or what?

The order of the speeches

The traditional order of toasts has a certain logic. The first speech leads up to a toast to the bride and bridegroom, the most important people of the day. In effect, at a traditional first wedding they are the honoured guests of the hosts, her parents. But while, as host, her father can make a speech or toast to his new son-in-law, it would be a bit immodest for him to sing the praises of his own daughter, so often a friend of the family is chosen to make a speech and toast to both bride and bridegroom, particularly if the father is going to speak later. The honour of making the first speech may go to the best speaker or the best friend, providing your choice keeps as many people as possible happy!

It falls to the bridegroom to reply to the first speech on behalf of himself and his bride. Whom should he thank? Both his in-laws, especially if they've paid for or organized the wedding, and especially his mother-in-law. Who else has helped? Presumably the bridesmaids. So he ends with a toast to the bridesmaids and/or Matron of Honour.

The bride, however, may speak instead of her husband or as well as him. If there are no bridesmaids the bridegroom can make a toast to his bride, who can speak next in reply. The bride can propose a toast to the bridegroom if the first toast was to her alone, or to the bridesmaids or Matron of Honour. Alternatively, she can propose a toast to the family of the bridegroom, or if they are not present, to the guests.

The best man replies on behalf of the helpers (the bridesmaids). If there are no bridesmaids he does not have to speak, though he may wish to do so. The best man or the bridegroom can end his speech with a toast to the hosts, and the bride's father or mother, or both, can reply.

An optional final toast to HM The Queen is made at most Jewish weddings in the UK. Lastly, the best man or the toastmaster reads the telegrams in full if there are only a few, or reads the wittiest in full and then gives just the names of the senders of the others if there are many.

Variations to these customs can be made when there are no bridesmaids, or parents, or for a second marriage where the couple are paying for their own wedding.

When you have decided who is speaking, tell them all how many speakers there are and in which order they are speaking. Also check whom they will be toasting. And, of course, let them all know as soon as possible so that they have plenty of time to prepare.

How to give a toast

At the end of your speech, lift your glass in the air and then wait for everybody to stand and raise their glasses. Once all noise has finished, you can then give the toast.

Surprise announcements

The surprise delivery of a large gift, or the surprise arrival of a friend or relative from overseas, can be great fun. However, the best man or chief bridesmaid will have to take responsibility for the announcement, and the safe-keeping of any gift. Most gifts are sent to the home of the bride's mother in advance. That way the donor's cards are not muddled in the confusion of the day, and presents are kept safely and not left in hotels or halls where they might go astray.

It is the bride's day, and surprise announcements of the engagements and forthcoming weddings of other guests might cause illwill. They could deflect attention from the bride. The announcement of the engagement of the bride's sister would be acceptable, but only if the bride herself knows in advance and gladly agrees to the public announcement being made at her wedding.

Language barriers

It can be a problem if, for example, the bridegroom speaks no English: either he, or the bride and the family, may feel he ought to have the opportunity to speak at his own wedding, or that he has a duty to honour his hosts by thanking them publicly.

There are two solutions. Either he speaks in his own language and an interpreter delivers a translation; the translator can be the bride or another person. Or he can remain silent except for nodding, smiling and lifting his glass, allowing the bride to speak on their behalf, making due reference to him – 'my husband has asked me', etc.

The same system will be adopted if you have two receptions, one in each country. The speakers just have to do everything twice, taking note of which family is playing host.

Informal receptions

If your wedding guests are not seated in a reception hall, but milling around a hotel or house your problem is to ensure that everyone is gathered in the right place at the right time to hear the speeches. You may have to tell guests in advance: 'We're cutting the cake and having the speeches in the dining room at half past', then send the chief bridesmaid into the gardens if it is a fine day, and the other bridesmaids around the house, to inform stragglers that the speeches are about to be made.

Don't start the proceedings until you are sure that the speakers themselves are present as well as the hosts and anyone else who will be thanked or mentioned in the speeches. Keep the speeches short because one-third of the audience can't see, one-third can't hear, and one-third are trying to locate a seat so that they will not drop their handbag, glass or plate, when they clap you.

Even if you decide to dispense with speeches altogether, you may find that after the cake is cut the crowd of well-wishers start chanting: 'Speech! Speech!', so that at least the bridegroom has to give a speech. Somebody will then decide to give an impromptu reply if the best man doesn't, which makes him feel he should have spoken. So if you are the best man, why not prepare a few words? You might then find that, having gone to the trouble of preparing a good speech and a joke just in case, you decide that you might as well give the speech anyway!

After the party

Souvenirs of the wedding may include photographs of the speakers delivering speeches, the guests around the happy couple with glasses raised, typed copies of the speech to go in the wedding album, or video recordings of the occasion.

When the party is over, members of the bridal party, and guests, may want to approach the speakers and personally thank them, complimenting them on a good, amusing speech. In addition, the bride and bridegroom, or hosts, could express thanks in the form of a short note and accompanying photo or small gift.

Following the honeymoon, a party is often held to show the family photos of the trip. At the same time if a video has been taken of the wedding the speakers will want to see themselves. Should they have made any small mistakes they will laugh and learn to improve next time, and if their performance was perfect they will be absolutely delighted.

Planning and preparing the speech

When first sitting down to write your speech it may be a good idea to ask yourself why you have been asked to speak. Is it because you are expected to express good wishes or thanks, or because you are old and wise and expected to give advice, or because you are an extrovert and known for being humorous, because you are closely related to other members of the family, or because you are a friend who has known the bride and bridegroom for many years? The answer to this question may suggest to you what sort of speech to give.

Planning your speech

It is important to leave yourself enough time before the wedding in order to give much consideration as to what you would like to say and to do any research necessary, as well as to write your speech and to perform any last-minute pruning. Remember, a few scribbled notes will not suffice.

Length of speech

It is important to decide the length of your speech before beginning to research and write it. Too short and it may seem rude, too long and it may bore the guests and dampen the proceedings. If you really can't decide, settle on about five minutes. As a rule of thumb, if the occasion is a very formal one it will demand a longer speech; an informal occasion is more flexible. Remember, your speech will reflect not only on those you are speaking about, but upon yourself.

Gathering information

Before even attempting to write your speech, take stock of the information you have to hand and see where the gaps occur. Only then should you set about researching in order to fill your speech out, make it interesting, witty, or whatever style of speech you would like to make. Beware, however, of drowning yourself in pages of notes. Panic will not be too far away if, having collected all your information, you have only a little time to write the speech.

Begin your research by looking for ideas on which you can expound and expand. For instance, the theme of marriage itself is always popular. You could research ideas on the history of marriage and interesting marriage customs both here and abroad.

In addition, you could ask the parents of the bride and bridegroom about their marriages. Did the marriage take place in wartime? Wearing similar clothes? With hundreds of guests? Enquire about the cake, photographer, transport, food, music, dancing, honeymoon destination, and first home. The grandparents, uncles and aunts may also have interesting stories about their weddings and the marriages of friends, brothers, sisters and other relatives that took place in unusual or typically different circumstances in earlier days.

The best time to get people to talk about themselves is when you are sitting around the table over a meal or having tea, and when they are relaxed and are not likely to be diverted by other activities. Remember here that some people do not like seeing you write down their words, since it interrupts their flow of thought. If you have a poor memory you could slip away for a moment and write yourself a quick note. Alternatively, use a small tape recorder so that you can join in the conversation without note-taking. Reactions to tape recording differ. While a few people do not like tape recorders, others love to have what they said played back at a family party, and then argue and correct each other and make interesting extra comments.

From the family history you can learn about the family's ancestors, where they have lived and worked, where they met, their education, work skills, achievements, hobbies and character. Personal anecdotes can be added. You will need to strike a balance between personal and general remarks. For example, if the bride and bridegroom have fascinating family histories, it would be unfortunate if you generalized a great deal and delivered a speech that could have been given at anybody's wedding.

So make sure you persist even if your first enquiry produces no immediate result. You may find that the bride says: 'Don't bother to say anything about where I went to school and where we met. It's not really interesting.' If one of your subjects doesn't provide you with information, ask another. You might discover that someone else such as the bride's mother has really interesting revelations about the bride. Maybe despite or because of failing 'O' levels, she went on to become the first woman engineer at her college because her earlier setbacks had made her determined to prove that she could succeed.

Make enquires from both sides of the family. The discovery of the meaning of the family name may be news to the other side. And the countries all the grandparents came from could be quite interesting. But so is the fact that one or both families have lived in the same area for four generations. This is not the sort of news that would make the front pages of newspapers, but you can assume that on the day everyone will be interested in the bride and bridegroom and their respective families.

The profession of the bride or bridegroom may provide speech matter. If your subject has academic qualifications you could ask such questions as: 'How long did it take you to get your degree?'; 'What subject is your PhD in?'; 'How long have you been a member of the Architect's Association'; 'Where did you study for the Bar?'; 'How does the FBOA differ from the FSMC?'.

If the bride or bridegroom, or their families or ancestors, are famous, it might be worth your while looking them up in *Who's Who*, and similar reference works, of which there are many editions covering authors, scientists, theatrical personages and royalty.

Composing and pruning your speech

There is detailed information in Chapter Three about how you should set about writing your speech, but for a wedding or other family occasion there are certain additional points to be aware of.

Work out the structure

- Prune your notes if necessary and arrange them in the correct order. List the essentials to be included such as thanks and the toast. Then consider your opening remarks.

- Avoid stereotyped ideas if possible. Have you talked only about the bride cooking for the bridegroom when you know she is a career girl and a women's libber, and even if she is not, some of the audience could be?

- Delete anything in dubious taste. If in doubt, leave it out. Avoid negatives, regrets, criticisms of others, making the families or yourself appear foolish and anything vague.

- Remove rude jokes and deliberate sexual innuendos, and watch out for unintended double entendres that might make inebriated members of the audience laugh when you are being serious and sincere. You can cause hysterics all round with such apparently innocent remarks as the bride's father saying: 'I didn't expect to enjoy myself so much. You don't enjoy things so much when you get older.'

Reading your speech aloud

Read the speech aloud to yourself first to be sure the sentences are not too long and you are not stumbling over them. It must sound like something you would say spontaneously. Later when you are satisfied, you might read it to a limited number of people – just one or two. You don't want all the wedding party to have heard the speech in advance of the wedding.

Improving the style

Change words or phrases you have repeated. Enliven clichés by subtly altering them if possible. Explain jargon and foreign phrases.

Change repetitions by looking for new words with the same meaning in a thesaurus. There are many different editions of these available fairly cheaply from bookshops. A dictionary of synonyms and antonyms might also be useful. And if you intend to compose your own poems, limericks or verses, a songwriter's rhyming dictionary would be invaluable.

For an ordinary wedding, a colloquial way of speaking will be suitable. However, should you be called upon to speak at a grand, formal wedding you may feel that a more erudite speech is required. Forms of address and titles for important personages can be found in reference books.

To eliminate or locate colloquial words there are dictionaries of slang. For transatlantic marriages, several dictionaries of American expressions are available, enabling you to eliminate Americanisms, explain yourself to American listeners, or make jokes about the differences between Americanisms and conventional English language.

Anticipating little problems

Try to anticipate any controversial subjects and disasters you might have to mention, or avoid mentioning, in the course of your speech.

Make yourself a troubleshooter's checklist. What would I say if:

- Her father had recently died?

- His or her parents couldn't or didn't attend?

- The best man didn't arrive because his plane from India was delayed?

- It turned out to be the bridegroom's second wedding, although it is the bride's first?

- The chief bridesmaid didn't turn up because she was ill?

- The bridegroom dried up and forgot to compliment the bridesmaids so I couldn't thank him?

- You may also have to state facts that are obvious to you, but would not be to distant cousins.

Final check

Finally, check that your speech fits in with the speeches and toasts given by others. Be sure that you know the name of the previous speaker so that you can say: 'Thank you, George', confident that his name is not James. And if your friend, the bridegroom, or the bride's father-in-law or another older man is usually called 'Al', on this occasion should you be calling him by his full name (and if so, is that short for Albert, Alfred, Ali, Alexis, Alexander) or, even more formally, Mr Smith?

**RUN A FEW QUESTIONS PAST YOURSELF
ABOUT YOUR SPEECH:**

• Will everyone understand and appreciate the content?

• Will the guests have heard all my jokes before?

• Will my speech give offence or repeat what others
  have said?

• Did people laugh/fall asleep during the rehearsal?

• Do I know my speech well enough?

• Have I worked out how long it will last?

Delivering your speech

Detailed information on delivering your speech will be found
in Chapter Four, but here are a few additional points about
using a microphone, with particular relevance for weddings.
(See also page 124.)

Using a microphone

When you arrive at the wedding reception check whether a
microphone will be available. But be prepared and able to
speak without it just in case it is not available or an electrical
fault develops.

At a seated dinner the speakers are usually at the top table and the microphone is nearby and can be handed to each speaker. But if the first speaker is not seated at the top table there may be a pause while he walks to the microphone. If a delay occurs between one speaker and the next the audience may start talking so that the next speaker will have to recapture their attention. A toastmaster has his own techniques. He may bang on the table with a mallet and then shout: 'Pray silence for THE BRIDEGROOM!'

The first speaker should not be the one who discovers whether the microphone is working or not. Perhaps the best man could take on the responsibility of arriving before the guests and checking the microphone. However, the best man is sometimes asked to stay behind at the church, organizing transport and ensuring that the last guest does not get stranded when all the cars have departed. In this case another usher or bridesmaid could take over the duty of checking the microphone.

The usual technique for checking that the microphone is set to the correct level after the audience arrives is to call: 'Can you all hear me?' Since those at the front shout loudly, you won't necessarily know that those at the back can't. A more interesting variation would be: 'Hello, I'm going to check that the microphone works before I start. Could those on the back table shout, 'Hello'.' Another variation would be: 'Hello, I just want to check you all got here all right. Did the relatives from Manchester arrive?' (Check the table plan in advance to see who is on the back table or tables.) 'Yes? Good. Now I can start.'

When you begin speaking into the microphone, start softly and then speak louder. You don't want to start by bellowing so loudly that people shrink in alarm. If you see the audience cowering back, you are too loud. Alternatively, see if they are straining to hear you. Some experienced speakers ask a friend to stand against the back wall and signal with hands facing forward by their ears if you need to speak louder, and with hands horizontal if you should speak more softly.

Ensure that you are not so near the microphone that it picks up every sound, including heavy breathing and muttered asides. Neither stand so far away that it cannot pick up your voice. The other thing to avoid is swaying backward and forward so that you are alternately bellowing and whispering, fading out or disappearing entirely at intervals like a badly tuned radio station!

Don't be frightened by hearing the sound of your own voice magnified. Everybody wants to hear you because they are your friends, or because they are friends of the happy couple and want to hear what you have to say about them. If you practise listening to yourself speaking on tape, you will be used to the timbre or magnification of your voice.

Pre-wedding speeches

Various kinds of engagement and pre-wedding parties can be held. An engagement party is arranged to introduce families and friends to the other families, and inform everyone that the young couple are now attached. If the engagement period is to be protracted because the couple are young or studying, there may be a big party not unlike a small-scale version of the wedding at which the future bride has a chance to display her ring to well-wishers and acquire presents for the new home, for which the guests must be thanked.

More than one bride's father has been heard to say that he did not want to have a large engagement party if the wedding was to follow within a year because that would involve him in the organization and expense of 'two weddings'. That is why the bridegroom's family traditionally hosts the engagement party, but there is no reason why one should not be held by the bride's family, or by both families in their own home or elsewhere, particularly if the two families live in different areas.

Unlike wedding reception speeches, the engagement party speeches are usually very short, merely introducing the young couple, expressing pleasure at the engagement and wishing them happiness. A parent of the bride or bridegroom speaks or, if there are no parents present, another older relative playing host can make the speech.

Engagement party speeches

Speech to the happy couple by the bridegroom's (or the bride's) father/mother:

'I am delighted to welcome you to meet Steven's fiancée Annabelle and her family [*or Annabelle's fiancé Steven and his family*]. They hope to marry next June, or sooner if they find a house. It is lovely to see you all, and so many friends from their old school and college and Steven's office [*or from Annabelle's old school*]. I hope everybody's got a glass of champagne because I would like you to join me in wishing every happiness to Annabelle and Steven. [*Pause*]
To Annabelle and Steven.'

Reply and thanks to the host and guests by bride/ bridegroom and toast to the other family:

'I want to thank Mum and Dad for throwing this lovely party so that you could meet Annabelle and her family [*or Steven and his family*]. Thank you all for coming this evening, and for bringing such generous presents. I'd like you to drink a toast to Annabelle's parents, Betty and Jim [*or Steven's parents, John and Clare*]. [*Pause*]
To Betty and Jim [*or John and Clare*].'

Thanks and toast to hosts by the other family:

'I'd like to thank Betty and Jim for organizing this wonderful party to give both of our families the ideal opportunity to get to know each other.'

Bachelor parties

Stag and hen parties used to be held the night before the wedding, the last opportunity for the girls and boys to go out with friends of their own sex. Now, however, the occasionally unfortunate results of these parties have made it unpopular to hold them immediately before the wedding, and instead a date a couple of weeks earlier is chosen.

The responsibility of the brother, sister or best friend who organizes the bachelor party is to ensure that it is a happy event for the guest of honour, and that the speeches, jokes, entertainment and gifts do not embarrass those present or others absent who will hear about the party later, or imperil the relationship between the engaged couple. Organizing the event successfully, making an amusing speech, and getting the right balance between outrageous fun and good taste will indicate to the bride or bridegroom that you can be relied upon to perform well as best man or bridesmaid at the subsequent wedding.

Bachelor and hen party speeches

Speech to bridegroom-to-be by best friend:

'We are here to say goodbye to our brother, Steven, who is departing for the land of the married. We all knew that Steven was regarded as an eligible bachelor, but we didn't think that marriage was what he was eligible for. We tried to dissuade Steven from marrying, but alas to no avail. We warned him that a husband is a glorified handyman, that he will be spending his weekends painting, decorating, gardening and maintaining the car. He will be abandoning happy Saturday afternoons spent watching football, and instead spend them shopping. If he cannot afford a dishwasher, he will be a dishwasher. Sunday will no longer be a day of rest spent playing cricket or sailing, but devoted to visiting in-laws. Evenings at the pub or the bar will have to be abandoned and he will stay at home, opening bottles for others to drink. To all this, he said, and I quote: 'Rubbish.' So you see, his vocabulary has changed already! He continued: 'You are not married. How do you know?'

So we sought wiser men than ourselves who have trodden the same path he proposes to take. W.C. Fields said that women are like elephants, very nice to look at, but he wouldn't want to own one. A look at our former friends who have married will show that marriages are made in heaven above, to make life hell below.' [*Alternatively choose a quotation from the selection in Chapter Eight.*] Many young ladies will mourn Steven's departure. Sometimes they were queuing up to speak to him. In fact, a lady who looked like Britney Spears [*or other celebrity the groom is known to admire*] was hiding in the phone box at the car park waiting to see him as we came along tonight. She is still waiting, alas in vain.

We, too, have failed. He remains unconvinced. To him, an evening with one woman, Annabelle, is worth an evening with ten of us. She must be a truly wonderful girl. We shall never know. So we have gathered here this evening to spend a last evening telling jokes with our friend, who is unfettered by responsibilities. We decided to present him with a small token that he can take to his new life, and keep in memory of his bachelor days and the friends he has left behind. Unfortunately, when we went into the shop to buy his gift we met a couple of his ex-girlfriends who insisted on coming along to remind him of the girls he is leaving behind, and to present him with a small, but wonderfully packaged gift, a token of our friendship. Steven – here they are!'

At this stage, two male friends dressed in drag appear, possibly as twin brides, preferably in long dresses or other outfits that keep them well covered to prevent any incidents among their own group or from outsiders. They present the gift.

Reply and thanks by the bridegroom-to-be:

'Dear Friends. I appreciate your concern for me. I, too, am concerned for you. Your gifts are very welcome and will be appreciated by Annabelle as well as myself. Boys [*Guys/Mates*], you don't know what you are missing. While I am tucked up by my warm fire being waited on hand and foot, you will be out in your cars touring the streets with nowhere to go, wishing in vain for a lovely girl to console you and end your loneliness.

How can a football or a golf ball be compared to a girl? Those of you who still do not know the difference, I hope will one day find out. In only five weeks I shall be marrying Annabelle. We look forward to seeing you all at our wedding, and later to welcoming you to dinner in our new home. Who knows, at the wedding or at our place you may meet the girl who may change your mind about the joys of remaining a bachelor.

Annabelle and I have got a 'little list' of eligible bachelors, and you are all on it. We have had many good times together, and we shall have more. I am not halving my friends, but doubling them. Please raise your glass and drink a toast to Alan who has organized this party for me. May he enjoy happy bachelor days, but not too many, before he realizes the error of his ways and is claimed by his own beautiful lady. [*Pause*] To Alan.' [*An alternative toast could be to friendships that endure forever.*]

Speech to bride-to-be by best friend:

'We tried to dissuade Annabelle from marrying, but alas to no avail. We warned her that a wife's work is never done. She is chained to the kitchen sink and washing socks. Unpaid secretary, social organizer, babysitter, cook, etc. When we told her this she said, and I quote: 'Phooey!'

There are many young men who will mourn her departure from the ranks of the available, ah [*sigh*], some of whom had fond memories of her, others, merely hopes. She was a very popular girl. Men flocked into her office. We realized why when we called. She had taken the sign MEN from the gents and put it on her office door. But now that Steven has claimed her, those days are gone. Her parents and flatmates look forward to the recovery of their telephones and bathrooms.

We must admit that it looks to us like a very good match, and it is only because she is marrying Steven that she has such an idealized view of what men and marriage are really like. Does she not know the truth, that after marriage, life changes. Men can be late. Women cannot. We are duty bound to warn her of what others who married have said. But since we have failed to persuade her to stay single, we can only wish her well, and give her this small token of our good wishes for her future, in memory of our happy single days together.' [*Produce appropriate gift.*]

Reply and thanks by the bride-to-be:

'Dear friends. I appreciate your message of goodwill, and your charming gifts. Don't you dare tell Steven that you found this *pair of men's underpants/bottle of tequila/Michael Jackson record* under my bed! I shall always remember you, the way you look tonight! We have had a lot of fun together and we still shall. You'll all be at my wedding in six weeks/six months time, and frequent guests at my house, and in my garden. I shall throw my bouquet to one of you at the wedding and who knows, there might be another wedding in the not too distant future for somebody. My mother says there's one for everyone. Let's all have a drink together, I hope all my girlfriends will meet steady boyfriends, but as Helen organized this party and is going to be my chief bridesmaid, I'd like to wish happiness to Helen. To Helen.' [*An alternative toast would be: 'To friendship. May good friends stay together forever'.*]

Wedding Speeches

The following sample speeches are to suit different situations and speakers. Choose the most appropriate speech and substitute your own details. Alternatively, pick up a pen and a piece of paper and compose your own speech immediately after reading all these for inspiration.

Toasts to the bride and bridegroom

Brief toast at an informal wedding party:

'I would like to propose a toast to Annabelle and Steven, wishing them much joy and happiness for their future together. [*Pause*] To Annabelle and Steven!'

Brief, simple, direct speech for the bride's father:

'Reverend Brown, Ladies and Gentlemen, all my guests [*pause*], I cannot tell you how pleased I am today to see my daughter Annabelle looking so happy, as she begins life as the wife of Steven. My wife and I do not feel that we are losing Annabelle, but entrusting her to Steven's good care. As we have got to know him better, he has shown himself to be exactly the sort of person we had hoped Annabelle would marry – charming, sincere, reliable – with a clear idea of what he wants from life and how to achieve it. I know that his many friends and family, as well as those who have only recently met him, think that this must be one of those marriages that are made in heaven, and will want to join me in wishing Steven and Annabelle a long and happy married life together.

So please stand and raise your glasses, and drink to the health and happiness of Annabelle and Steven. [*Pause*] To Annabelle and Steven!'

Longer, personalized speech by an old friend or relative when bride's father is present, but does not make a speech:

'Annabelle's parents have done me the honour of offering me the opportunity to make a speech on this wonderful occasion and propose a toast to Annabelle and Steven. When I asked why they chose me, George said: 'Because you are the President of the Oxford Drama Club [*my bank manager/ my oldest friend/the boss/have known us 25 years/the tallest/have the loudest voice*]', and Martha said: 'Because you have known Annabelle since she was fourteen [*a baby/a child/all her life/at school/at college/you tell the best jokes*].'

I have seen Annabelle acting [*in school plays/at the drama club*] on many occasions, and today she has a starring role.

Over the years I have seen her develop many talents and accomplishments. She has won prizes for [*drama/music/ essay-writing/cookery/coming top of her class in school*], been awarded the first grade in [*drama/music*], studied [*whatever is appropriate*], learned how to [*drive/ski/sail/ swim/dance/surf*] and followed her interests in [*whatever is appropriate*], as well as finding time to [*raise money for charity/do voluntary work with handicapped children/attend church functions regularly/design clothes/paint/draw*] and help in her family's [*shop/business/company/restaurant*].

It was while she was at [*school/college/work*], that she met Steven who was [*studying/working/travelling*]. Though Steven had not yet [*qualified as a doctor/passed his 'A'' levels/ learnt to tell the difference between a gasket and a sprocket*], it was obvious that they had much in common.

[*Or*: 'At first it didn't look as if they had much in common. But as they got to know each other Annabelle discovered that Steven liked [*the arts as much as the sciences/hiking as well as driving/driving cars as well as repairing them*]. And Steven learned that Annabelle could [*pilot a plane/ice a cake/run a playgroup/speak fluent French*]. And when Steven learned that [*Annabelle/Annabelle's father/mother/ brother*] was [*an MP/barrister/had the best collection of Beatles records*], that clinched it.']

These young people have a bright future ahead of them, a wonderful [*career/job/home*] planned in London [*New York/Sydney*]. And I am sure you will want to join me in wishing them every success and happiness in their new venture and marriage. Please raise your glasses and drink to the health and prosperity of Annabelle and Steven. [*Pause*] To Annabelle and Steven!'

Speech by relative/friend when the bride's father is recently deceased:

'It is my great pleasure to be here with you on this happy occasion and to help Annabelle and Steven celebrate their marriage. I have known Annabelle and her parents for many years, since [*I/we/they*] came to live in [*name of city*].

Annabelle's late father, George, used to enjoy [*a game of football/a game of golf/fixing the car on Saturday afternoons*], and we spent many happy hours together [*sailing/relaxing*] often accompanied by Steven. I remember George saying that Steven seemed to be a very [*pleasant/ good-natured/hard-working/ambitious/talented*] young man. They got on well and George would have been delighted to have seen this happy day. Although we miss George's presence, and his unfailing good humour, we know that he was looking forward to this wedding and we have fulfilled his hopes and wishes, and in a sense he is with us here today in our memories of him.

He would have been very satisfied to know what a comfort Steven has been to our family, how understanding, how supportive a friend in time of need, a valuable help to us in everything from fixing the car, taking over day to day decisions affecting [*the business/work/Annabelle's job*], to just being there when we wanted advice and assistance. The wedding was postponed, but Annabelle is a girl well worth waiting for. Doesn't she look a picture today? George would have been proud of her, as I am sure Steven is. And it is with every confidence that I tell you I am sure that this young couple will have a very happy marriage, and I ask you to join me in wishing them both a long, happy and prosperous future together. Please stand and lift your glasses. I propose a toast – to Annabelle and Steven. [*Pause*]
To Annabelle and Steven!'

Speech suitable for an older man addressing a large, distinguished audience:

'Ladies and Gentlemen [*pause*], it is always a pleasure to attend a wedding. They say that the world loves a lover and I think this is true. Marriage is the expression of love, and also the start of a lifelong adventure. Plato said: 'The beginning is the most important part of the work.' If that is the case, then Annabelle and Steven have been fortunate in enjoying the most wonderful beginning. They already have most of the good gifts one would wish upon a young couple. Annabelle is a beautiful bride, Steven is a handsome husband, and both come from secure family homes where their parents have set examples of what a good marriage should be.

A good marriage is not something you can create on your own without help from your partner. It is a joint venture. Marriage is like a journey in a boat. You cannot drill a hole in the boat and when water floods in say to your companion: 'It's nothing to do with me, the water is coming in on your side of the boat.' You must row in the same direction. In fact, love has been defined as not looking at each other, but looking in the same direction.
If marriage is a boat, then many of us are in the same boat! Annabelle and Steven, you are embarking on a wonderful journey, and you have many friends who will support you, and help you, and wish you well. I would now like to ask everyone in this room to stand with me, and raise their glasses. I propose a toast to the long life, health, wealth and happy marriage of Annabelle and Steven. [*Pause*]
To Annabelle and Steven!'

Best man's toast to bride and bridegroom

Impromptu speech at a very small wedding without bridesmaids:

'This is a lovely small, intimate gathering of friends, which is the way Annabelle and Steven wanted it to be. And we all appreciate how honoured we are to be among the select few who they have chosen to share this special occasion with them. Everyone here is a close friend or relative and we all have personal knowledge of Annabelle's unique qualities, her kindness, her gift for creating a happy atmosphere and her loyal friendship. And we are delighted that she is marrying Steven, who is so [*loved/admired*] by his family and close friends and is respected by all of us for his [*hard work/ talents/skills/zest for life*]. He shares many of her good qualities and they both deserve all the good things in life. So let's wish them both a very happy married life together. Has everyone got a drink? Good. [*Pause*]
To Annabelle and Steven.'

An alternative could be:

'It gives me special pleasure to be present at the wedding of my good friends Annabelle and Steven, because I introduced them at [*name of the venue*] and because I have known both of them for many years at [*school/the tennis club*]. May their lives continue with equal joy and may they share many happy occasions and reunions such as this with our families and friends. Here's to Annabelle and Steven. [*Pause*]
To Annabelle and Steven.'

Toast to the bride's parents

Bridegroom's speech, replying to first toast to bride and bridegroom, a longer, humorous speech:

'Reverend Brown, Ladies and Gentlemen [*pause*], thank you very much, George, for those kind words. It goes almost without saying how pleased I am to be here today. In order not to dull your pleasure I intend to speak for only a few minutes in case we all [*get snowed in/melt away in the heat*]! We couldn't have wished for better weather – [*perfect sunshine, just the right start for a marriage/a beautiful, romantic white Christmas*].

As you all know, Annabelle has been a much sought-after girl, but I'm pleased to announce the winner of the competition – me. There are no runners up, or associated prizes.

My new mother-in-law, Martha, has worked long and hard for many months to prepare this wonderful occasion, all the little details such as these beautiful [*flowers/cake decorations*] were planned by her, and my father-in-law has taken on his second mortgage without complaint, like the good-natured man he is. I am very pleased to be part of their family and to know that my parents feel the same.

Speaking of whom, today represents a great occasion for both my parents, being the culmination of many years of planning of a different sort. They have prepared me well, supported me through university and taught me the difference between right and wrong, so that I know which I am enjoying at any given time!

Annabelle is beautiful, intelligent and hard working. The list of her good qualities is extremely long. Unfortunately I cannot read her handwriting.

I would like to thank you all for your presence – in both senses of the word, but especially for the smiling faces I see in front of me. I am particularly pleased that Aunt Alice managed to make the long journey down to Surrey from Aberdeen for this occasion, and we are all delighted that Annabelle's sister, Sharon, flew all the way from Australia to join us and be such a charming bridesmaid. Of course, she had a 'little help' – quite a big help, actually, from Tracey, who looked so sweet holding Annabelle's train.

My best man, Alan, has made everything go smoothly, and I appreciate his contribution to what has been a perfect day.

Finally, I must pay tribute to the bridesmaids Sharon, Natalie, Margaret and Sue, whose invaluable support has helped to make this day so successful.'

If there are no bridesmaids, the toast is to his parents-in-law as follows:

'In conclusion, thank you, everybody, for listening, and I hope you are having a wonderful [*afternoon/evening*] and are all as happy as we are today. Would you kindly stand and raise your glasses and drink a toast to the health of your hosts, two wonderful people, George and Martha. [*Pause*]
To George and Martha!'

Toast to bridegroom and both families

Informal toast by the bride:

'I'd like to propose a toast to the most wonderful man in the world, my new husband Steven. I'd also like to thank his parents for what they have contributed over the years to make him the person he is, supporting him through college, and also for making me such a welcome member of their family. I must also thank my parents for everything they have done for me and especially this wonderful event, my wedding to Steven. May we all meet on many more happy occasions. [*Pause*] To Steven.'

Toast to the bridesmaids

Bridegroom's speech in reply to toast to the bride and bridegroom, a brief but sincere speech:

'My wife and I [*pause for laughter*] thank you for your kind words. It is wonderful to be surrounded by so many friends and good wishes. We have been overwhelmed by the kindness and help we have received, the generous gifts, and the people who have made extra contributions on this, our special day. I must mention the bridesmaids who have done so much to help my wife, and added glamour to the photographs that will remind us of this very happy occasion. [*Pause*] To the bridesmaids!'

Toast to the bridegroom's family

Reply by the bride's father to the bridegroom's toast to the bride's parents, who are hosts, giving personal family marriage details:

'Thank you, Steven. As you know Annabelle is our only daughter so this will be our only chance to stage what has been a lovely wedding. And we did not want to miss the opportunity of having such a wonderful day, complete with the white wedding car. When my parents' generation were marrying back in the Second World War, wedding couples needed clothing coupons from all their relatives to make the wedding dress and wedding suits, all of which had to be of sensible material so that they could be worn again. Everybody saved all their food coupons for the wedding cake. Since you could not go abroad, you honeymooned on the south coast at resorts such as Bournemouth where there was barbed wire on the beaches. For each generation the circumstances are different. Today, guests have flown in from [*Australia/America/France*] to be with Annabelle and Steven – something that would have been very rare sixty years ago. We have a photographer visiting us to make a video, so that we can remember this magical day for the rest of our lives, and all the wedding photos will be able to be digitally altered to hide my bald patch!

We want Annabelle and Steven to enjoy the things we never had, not to take them for granted, but to appreciate how lucky they are to be able to celebrate like this surrounded by their families and friends.

I know that Steven's parents understand how glad we are to do whatever we can for our daughter, and their son. We are very pleased to have Gregory and Gillian and their family here to celebrate with us. Their generous support and presence, joining in enthusiastically with everything we planned, has enabled us to truly enjoy this day. So please join me in drinking a toast to the health of my son-in-law's parents, Gregory and Gillian. [*Pause*] To Gregory and Gillian.'

Second weddings

Today, second weddings are increasingly common (around 40% of people marrying in the UK have firsthand experience of the proceedings), but it is important to remember that it is still a special occasion for all involved and may indeed be a first wedding for one of the partners. Try to be upbeat and positive in your speech and avoid too much talk of the couple's past or marital history. Don't dwell, even in jest, on the fact that the first marriage did not work. It may be appropriate to pay tribute to a former or ex-wife or husband. Perhaps he or she sadly died. Make sure you check this first with a close family member. Don't spring unknowns on the bride and bridegroom or their entourage. Be tactful, sensitive and discreet.

Your role is not to highlight that this is a second union, but to welcome all present, to embrace and bring together all the guests and family members in order to celebrate the special event. The strategy is inclusion not exclusion. There may be some fragile or delicately balanced relationships between families and individuals among those assembled – your role is to bridge any chasms, not highlight any gulfs. Don't tread on anyone's toes or you will want to hotfoot it out of there. And if there are children from either or both sides, make sure you include them in the toast, having checked with the bride or bridegroom about any sensitive areas.

Toasts to bride and bridegroom (second marriage)

Speech by best man at a second wedding:

'I think I speak for everyone in this room when I say how happy I am to see Stephen and Mary married – at last. And I say 'at last' because this is a second marriage for both of them, and they truly deserve this and every future moment of happiness, of which we wish them an endless number. Every wedding is special, but this one is doubly so. Stephen and Mary were tailor-made for each other – a perfect match, as we can all see today. Both are courageous (as today's second foray into the conjugal jungle proves!), they complement each other, in both senses of the word, and they are committed, compassionate and caring (all the 'c' words men usually avoid!). Not only did they embrace each other, but they also embraced each other's children, relatives, friends, hopes, fears and dreams. Today, we celebrate not only the union of two people of whom we are all so fond, but also two families, two lives and two futures. And it would not have been such a wonderful day without the beautiful bridesmaids and page boys [*toast by name*] and the wonderful hard work and organization by all those responsible [*toast by name*]. Let's raise our glasses now to the beautiful, blissful bride and the gorgeous groom with the biggest grin in the world. Ladies

and gentlemen, please charge your glasses. [*Pause*]
I give you Stephen and Mary.

Short, happy, slightly humorous speech for a bride enjoying her first marriage to a divorced man:

'Annabelle, for you this is a first marriage and a time of excitement and hope. For Steven it is a second marriage. He liked marriage so much that despite all the difficulties of his first attempt, when he met you he decided to try it again. Annabelle, you may not realize it, but you are gaining the advantage of marrying a man who has had the sharp corners rubbed off him. A mature specimen. A vintage blend.

We hope that you will always enjoy life together, a very long and happy life together, and that you will always retain the enthusiasm of this new start, and remember the joy and delight of finding each other, which is so evident today. So we will all raise our glasses to you and toast your future. [*Pause*]
To Annabelle and Steven.'

Short, happy, slightly humorous speech when the bridegroom is marrying for the first time, to a divorced woman:

'Steven, for you this is a first marriage and a time of expectation and hope. For Annabelle it is a second marriage. You must be especially proud today, because she liked you so much that despite all the difficulties of her first marriage, when she met you she decided to try it again. What an honour!

Annabelle, you have the advantage of experience. Steven, you may not realize it, but you are gaining many advantages by marrying a mature woman. Vintage. We hope that both of you will always enjoy married life, a very long and happy life together. And that you will always retain the enthusiasm of this new start and remember the joy and delight of finding each other, which is so evident today. So we will all raise our glasses to you and toast your future. [*Pause*]
To Annabelle and Steven.'

Sincere speech by a friend at a second or third marriage where both parties have been divorced or widowed at least once.

(*Select part, or all, of the following paragraphs, according to whether the parties have been recently widowed/divorced or alone for many years.*)

'All marriages are special occasions, but a second marriage is a doubly precious time because you do not take everything for granted. You realize how very lucky you are to be given another chance to be happy, and appreciate the blessing you have received in finding a soulmate and companion you can trust. It is a time of renewed hope.

I know that the two of you who are getting married today feel it is wonderful to be with so many good friends, and in particular one good friend, who understands your heartaches as well as your joys. That is so important.

It is a pleasure for you to experience an end to loneliness and sadness, and a joy for us to be witnesses and share this beginning with you. When you have experienced past disappointments, hardship and disillusionment, you know you have been up and down on life's waves. And when you are in the troughs of those waves, you sometimes wonder when you will ever come up again. Yet there is always a chance anew, an opportunity to feel love for someone, just like the first time. The past does not burden the present – but you learn by it, and do not repeat your mistakes. You have an opportunity through experience for knowing better than anyone else what is at stake and how much effort it takes, and what a loss it is if you don't do everything you can to make your partner contented. How fortunate you are to have found yet another chance at happiness together, with a better understanding than most people of what you should do to make a successful marriage, and how much you will gain.

It is difficult late in life to put away the past, and start again, but you have all the means at your disposal to make a success of the venture. Everyone has the right to happiness, and should you have the chance to find happiness, whether you are someone young starting life again, or a grandmother, why not?

We are confident that you will now receive the joy you deserve, and we are really happy for you. I speak for everyone here when I say we wish you all the best, and hope that for you [*pause*] 'the best is yet to come'. So, Annabelle and Steven, we would like to drink a toast to your happy future together. [Pause]
To Annabelle and Steven.'

Same-sex marriages

Laws about same-sex marriages vary from place to place and change constantly. Same-sex unions are becoming more common, and you may find yourself invited to attend or speak at such an occasion in the future. You will have been chosen to speak because you are an understanding and sympathetic person who knows the couple well. It will be important to do your research about the guest list, the age range involved, any strong feelings or possible hostility and what the couple feel might not be appropriate or what they would particularly like you to say. Ask yourself a few questions about your speech before you run it past the couple, in order to ensure that it is not potentially offensive, negative or ambivalent. Make it a positive and inclusive speech, celebrating the occasion, bridging any differences there may be in the audience and embracing diversity. Speak from the heart, be straightforward, genuine and open-minded. Address everyone in the room, ensuring that each guest feels an important part of the celebration. Remember that this may well be the first gay or lesbian ceremony that some of the guests have attended.

Speech to the couple by the best man:

'Firstly, I would like to welcome every one of you here to this very special occasion. We are all celebrating a wonderful day, a day when John and Simon were able to pledge their love and commitment to each other in a formal context and in front of all those whom they love and are loved by. I wanted to give them a big round of applause during the ceremony, but why don't we do just that here and now!

Today is a significant occasion not only for John and Simon, but also for their families and friends, all of whom were able to witness and share in the joy of their union. It is a day when we celebrate diversity and tolerance, when we embrace and rejoice in individual choice, a day when we come together united by the same thoughts and hopes – that John and Simon enjoy a future filled with deep joy, good health and true friendship. They have brought happiness and joy to their friends and it is a pleasure to be able to return some of that today. Please join me in wishing them both a wonderful life together and pledging our commitment to them as their friends and family. [*Pause*]
To John and Simon!'

Reply by John:

'Thank you, David, for such a wonderful, eloquent and speech. Thank you for being our best man and for supporting us throughout our preparations for today, and for not forgetting the rings! Simon and I feel honoured to be surrounded by so many close friends and family, all of whom have wished us well on our wedding day and embraced our decision to be together with such generosity of spirit and tolerance. Most of all, I would like to thank our parents for everything they have done. Reaching this point was a challenge for us and for them, but with their help, support, love and concern and that of all our friends and relatives, we were able to fulfil our greatest wish and be formally united. Embracing the new is not always easy. But life is full of change and developments, without which we would move backwards instead of forwards as a society. So let's toast the future – ours and yours. To you, from us – all the joy in the world.'

Wedding speeches to avoid

Regardless of the specific nature of the occasion, there are certain things that you should always avoid saying when asked to give a speech at a wedding. Some of these are as follows:

Over-apologetic speech:

'I don't know why anyone picked me to give a speech. I've never given a speech in my life before. I'm sure you don't want a long speech, but I've tried to prepare something, and I hope it's all right. Anyway, I did make some notes somewhere [*silence*]. Well, I can't find them, but [*pause*], oh, here it is. I've got a joke! 'As I was on my way to the wedding' [*pause*]. Oh, I've dropped it! Can you move your chair? No, don't bother. It's not really funny and you've probably heard it anyway. Most of you don't know Alf, but I expect you'll want to wish him, and the bride of course, a happy, er, future.'

Negative speech – and rather too revealing!

'I don't like speeches and I didn't want to give a speech, but Martha insisted I should. I suppose there was nobody else. I'm not a good speaker so I'm not going to bore you by making a long speech. Annabelle's a nice girl. I went out with her for a long time before she decided to marry Steven, or he decided to marry her. So I suppose it's what she wanted and she's done the right thing. Anyway, they know each other pretty well, having been living together for two years now. They wouldn't have got married if she hadn't been pregnant, so the baby has done something good. I know her Mum's pleased. The baby's going to be a big change. Everyone says: 'May all your troubles be little ones.' Apart from that I don't suppose they'll have any troubles. Marriage won't be a big change for them as they'll be living in the same place, you know. So everything is going to be all right, more or less.

Er – what else am I supposed to say? If you haven't got a drink the bar's still open. Prices are a bit steep, but you don't go to weddings every day. We're going to pass the hat round later, buy some beer and go back to their place. Annabelle's shaking her head. What's the matter? Don't you want us to? Steve says it's all right. Anyway, if you can't afford the whisky and you haven't got any beer left, grab a glass of water. To Annabelle and Steven! Can I sit down now?'

Extremely brief reply from the bridegroom:

'Thank you.'

Depressing speech:

'Relatives and friends, the one person missing here today is, of course, Annabelle's father, and no day can be really happy without him with us. Though I have tried to take his place, it is mere formality. No-one can take his place. Our happiness would have been complete if he had been here. Alas, he is not. We miss his help and his advice, as a husband to Martha, and father to Annabelle. He made so many plans for this wedding. If only he could have seen Annabelle today ... [*breaks off*]. Has somebody got a handkerchief to give to Annabelle?'

Reluctant father-in-law's speech:

'We're very pleased to see Annabelle getting married, at last. When I first met Steven I didn't like him very much, because of his hair and his clothes and the fact that he didn't have a steady job, but now I've got to know him he doesn't seem too bad. All these are things that can be changed. I'm sure Annabelle could change him if she wanted to, but she seems to like him the way he is. We're sorry that his Mum, what's her name?, died, and that his Dad didn't come along with his new stepmother, but perhaps it's just as well. Anyway, um, where was I? Well, er, I think that's everything. Let's all have a drink. Was I supposed to toast somebody?'

Gushing speech:

'I am deeply honoured to be invited to this momentous and lavish occasion by my esteemed friends, Martha and George. It is a privilege to pay them this small token of respect. I am sure Martha will forgive me for saying that her very presence excites envy from others. Martha has always been admired for her brilliant elegance, the epitome of good taste. The evidence before our eyes is her faultless attention to detail in these exquisite flower decorations. It has been a day that commenced so stunningly with the horse and carriage procession, swept forward with the harmonious, soaring, musical arrangements at the wedding ceremony, and has culminated in the utter perfection of the gourmet dinner, all in keeping with what we have come to expect from the organizational abilities of one of the world's paragons. No woman on earth could have been a more devoted, exacting, wife and mother, and Annabelle has admirably followed her mother's fine example, having inherited flawless cover-girl looks, and demonstrating impeccable good manners. You will, I am quite sure, agree with me totally when I say, our beautiful, delectable Annabelle is irreplaceable, and we shall miss her dreadfully, when she departs across the skies to the beautiful tropical paradise that she will enhance immeasurably.'

Long pompous speech:

'Your Royal Highness, Ladies and Gentlemen, as a minister, judge and professor, I feel I am in a good position to speak about the history of marriage, its importance in society, and the duties of the married couple to each other and the wider community. First, the history of marriage [*continues*]...

Now, we shall continue with the sayings of the numerous venerable sages [*continues*]...

Well, I agreed not to speak for more than half an hour, but I see that I have been speaking for a little longer than forty-five minutes. I could continue considerably longer on this fascinating subject, in fact I have several pages of notes here if anybody wishes to come and ask me any questions. Unfortunately I am obliged to terminate at this stage, because someone has just passed me a note saying that the band has to depart at 11pm and it is now 10.30. So I will conclude by saying that [*continues*]...'

Readings at weddings

Some people feel awkward about expressing their feelings in public, but readings and poems are an ideal way to get around this problem, as well as adding variation, depth and interest.

Inevitably, older texts sound more formal but their beauty and elegance can enhance even the most informal of ceremonies, adding a note of dignity and seriousness, and emphasizing the importance of the occasion.

Although it is a matter of personal choice as to when the texts are read, the following would generally be considered appropriate during the marriage ceremony itself.

To express the depth of the bride or bridegroom's love for their partner:

Sonnets from the Portuguese 43
Elizabeth Barrett Browning (1806–61)

How do I love thee? Let me count the ways.
I love thee to the depth and breadth and height
My soul can reach, when feeling out of sight
For the ends of being and ideal grace.
I love thee to the level of everyday's
Most quiet need, by sun and candlelight.
I love thee freely, as men strive for right;
I love thee purely, as they turn from praise.
I love thee with the passion put to use
In my old griefs, and with my childhood's faith.

I love thee with a love I seemed to lose
With my lost saints – I love thee with the breath,
Smiles, tears, of all my life! – and, if God choose,
I shall but love thee better after death.

To emphasize that two is better than one:

Love's Philosophy
Percy Bysshe Shelley (1792–1822)

The fountains mingle with the river
And the rivers with the oceans,
The winds of heaven mix forever
With a sweet emotion;
Nothing in the world is single,
All things by a law divine
In one another's being mingle –
Why not I with thine?

See the mountain's kiss high heaven
And the waves clasp one another;
No sister-flower would be forgiven
If it disdain'd its brother:

And the sunlight clasps the earth,
And the moonbeams kiss the sea –
What are all these kissings worth,
If thou kiss not me?

To express the bridegroom's love for the bride and show that his future happiness depends on her:

He Wishes For The Cloths of Heaven
William Butler Yeats (1865–1939)

Had I the heavens' embroidered cloths,
Enwrought with golden and silver light,
The blue and the dim and the dark cloths
Of night and light and the half-light,
I would spread the cloths under your feet:
But I, being poor, have only my dreams;
I have spread my dreams under your feet;
Tread softly because you tread on my dreams.

To express how important the bride's happiness is to the groom:

The Passionate Shepherd to His Love
Christopher Marlowe (1564–93)

Come live with me and be my love,
And we will all the pleasures prove
That hills and valleys, dales and fields
And all the craggy mountains yields.
There we will sit upon the rocks,
Seeing the shepherds feed their flocks
By shallow rivers, to whose falls
Melodious birds sing madrigals.
And I will make thee beds of roses
With a thousand fragrant posies,

A cap of flowers and a kirtle
Embroidered all with leaves of myrtle;

A gown made of the finest wool,
Which from our pretty lambs we pull;
Fair lined slippers for the cold,
With buckles of the purest gold;

A belt of straw and ivy buds,
With coral-clasps and amber studs;
And if these pleasures may thee move,
Come live with me and be my love.
The shepherd swains shall dance and sing
For thy delight each May morning;
If these delights thy mind may move,
Then live with me, and be my love.

To emphasize that they will love each other through 'thick and thin':

From *The Sonnets*
William Shakespeare (1564–1616)

Shall I compare thee to a summer's day?
Thou art more lovely and more temperate:
Rough winds do shake the darling buds of May,
And summer's lease hath all too short a date:
Sometime too hot the eye of heaven shines,
And often is his gold complexion dimmed;
And every fair from fair sometime declines,
By chance or nature's changing course untrimmed;

But thy eternal summer shall not fade,
Nor lose possession of that fair thou owest;
Nor shall death brag thou wander'st in his shade,
When in eternal lines to time thou growest:
So long as men can breathe, or eyes can see,
So long lives this, and this gives life to thee.

.....

Let me not to the marriage of true minds
Admit impediments. Love is not love
Which alters when it alteration finds,
Or bends with the remover to remove:
O, no! it is an ever-fixed mark,
That looks on tempests and is never shaken;
It is the star to every wandering barque,
Whose worth's unknown, although his height be taken.
Love's not time's fool, though rosy lips and cheeks
Within his bending sickle's compass come;
Love alters not with his brief hours and weeks,
But bears it out even to the edge of doom.
If this be error and upon me proved,
I never writ, nor no man ever loved.

On the nature of love:

From *The Prophet*, on love
Kahlil Gibran (1883–1931)

Love has no other desire but to fulfil itself.
But if you love and must needs have desires, let these be
your desires:
To melt and be like a running brook that sings its melody to
the night.
To know the pain of too much tenderness.
To be wounded by your own understanding of love;
And to bleed willingly and joyfully.
To wake at dawn with a winged heart and give thanks for
another day of loving;
To rest at the noon hour and meditate love's ecstacy;
To return home at eventide with gratitude;
And then to sleep with a prayer for the beloved in your heart
and a song of praise on your lips.

**On the strength that comes from understanding between
a couple and the partnership of marriage:**

I Ching, The Book of Changes

But when two people are at one in their innermost hearts,
They shatter even the strength of iron or bronze.
And when two people understand each other in their
innermost hearts,
Their words are sweet and strong, like the fragrance of
orchids.

To express their happiness and the love the bride feels for her groom:

To My Dear And Loving Husband
Anne Bradstreet (c.1612–72)

If ever two were one, then surely we.
If ever man were loved by wife, then thee;
If ever wife was happy in a man,
Compare with me, ye woman, if you can.
I prize thy love more than whole mines of gold
Or all the riches that the East doth hold.
My love is such that rivers cannot quench,
Nor ought but love from thee, give recompense.
Thy love is such I can no way repay,
The heavens reward thee manifold, I pray.
The while we live, in love let's so persevere,
That when we live no more, we may live ever.

Readings for during the speeches

The following texts could be incorporated into the speeches made at the reception.

Best man or family member

On how love and friendship go hand in hand:

This Day I Married My Best Friend
Author Unknown

This day I married my best friend
The one I laugh with as we share life's wondrous zest,
As we find new enjoyments and experience all that's best.
The one I live for because the world seems brighter

As our happy times are better and our burdens feel much lighter.

The one I love with every fibre of my soul.
We used to feel vaguely incomplete, now together we are whole.

Advice to the couple:

From *Marriage Advice*
Jane Wells (c. 1886)

Never go to bed angry.
Let your love be stronger than your hate or anger.
Learn the wisdom of compromise, for it is better to bend a little than to break.
Believe the best rather than the worst.
People have a way of living up or down to your opinion of them.
Remember that true friendship is the basis for any lasting relationship.
The person you choose to marry is deserving of the courtesies
and kindnesses you bestow on your friends.

On the wonder of love:

The Most Wonderful Of All Things In Life
Sir Hugh Walpole (1884–1941)

The most wonderful of all things in life is the discovery of another human being with whom one's relationship has a growing depth, beauty and joy as the years increase. This inner progressiveness of love between two human beings is a most marvellous thing; it cannot be found by looking for it or by passionately wishing for it. It is a sort of divine accident, and the most wonderful of all things in life.

On the nature of marriage:

From *The Prophet*, on marriage
Kahlil Gibran (1883–1931)

Then Almitra spoke again and said, 'And what of Marriage, master?'
And he answered saying:
You were born together, and together you shall be forevermore.
You shall be together when white wings of death scatter your days.
Aye, you shall be together even in the silent memory of God.
But let there be spaces in your togetherness,
And let the winds of the heavens dance between you.
Love one another but make not a bond of love:
Let it rather be a moving sea between the shores of your souls.
Fill each other's cup but drink not from one cup.
Give one another of your bread but eat not from the same loaf.
Sing and dance together and be joyous, but let each one of you be alone,

Even as the strings of a lute are alone though they quiver
with the same music.

Give your hearts, but not into each other's keeping.
For only the hand of Life can contain your hearts.
And stand together, yet not too near together:
For the pillars of the temple stand apart,
And the oak tree and the cypress grow not in each other's
shadow.

Humorous readings

The following texts are more light-hearted or humorous and
so are ideal for including in the speeches at the reception.

Bride to the bridegroom

Yes, I'll Marry You
Pam Ayres [1947–]

Yes, I'll marry you, my dear,
And here's the reason why;
So I can push you out of bed
When the baby starts to cry.

To Keep Your Marriage Brimming
Ogden Nash (1902–71)

To keep your marriage brimming,
With love in the loving cup,
Whenever you're wrong admit it;
Whenever you're right shut up.

Best man or bridegroom

This is an old-fashioned take on the woman's role in marriage and the view that every man needs a wife to look after him, and should be used in a humorous context.

Wedding Song
Traditional verse

Now some people think it's jolly for to lead a single life,
But I believe in marriage and the comforts of a wife.
In fact you might have quarrels, just an odd one now and then,
It's worth your while a-falling out to make it up again.
[Chorus] Get a little table, then a little chair,
And then a little house in the corner of a square,
Get a little teapot and save a little tin,
But don't forget the cradle for to rock the baby in.
Now a married man has comforts where a single man has not,
His clothes is always mended and his meals is always hot.
No matter what your trouble is your wife'll pull you through,
So if you think of marriage, lads, I'll tell you what to do.
[Chorus]
A single man in lodgings can't have much delight,
For there's no-one to speak with him when he sits home at night,
Nothing to attract him or to pass his time away,
So he'll quickly find the difference if he listens what I say.
It's little use of asking a girl to marry you,
Unless you've got a little corner of the table too,
For a good wife loves to see you cosy, clean and nice,
So if you wish to marry, boys, I'll tell you what to do.
[Chorus]

Although any family member could read this 'recipe', or even the best man, it would be perfect for the mother of the bride. It could also be adapted to suit the couple, such as 2 kilos of DIY, 500 grams of mowing the lawn, 750 grams of delicious home cooking, etc.

A Good Wedding Cake
Author Unknown

4lb of love.
1lb butter of youth.
1/2lb of good looks.
1lb sweet temper.
1lb of blindness of faults.
1lb of self forgetfulness.
1lb of pounded wit.
1lb of good humour.
2 tablespoons of sweet argument.
1 pint of rippling laughter.
1 wine glass of common sense.
1oz of modesty.

Put the love, good looks and sweet temper into a well furnished house. Beat the butter of youth to a cream, and mix well together with the blindness of faults. Stir the pounded wit and good humour into the sweet argument, then add the rippling laughter and common sense. Work the whole together until everything is well mixed, and bake gently for ever.

Best man or family member

To wish the couple well:

The Blessing Of The Apaches
Author unknown

Now you will feel no rain,
For each of you will be shelter to the other.
Now you will feel no cold,
For each of you will be warmth to the other.
Now there is no more loneliness for you,
For each of you will be companion to the other.
Now you are two bodies,
But there is only one life before you.
May beauty surround you both in the journey ahead and
through all the years.
May happiness be your companion and your days be good
and long upon the earth.

These texts could also be used in the speeches at the reception.

On love:

Corinthians 13:4–8, The Bible

Love is patient and kind; love is not jealous or boastful; it is
not arrogant or rude. Love does not insist on its own way; it
is not irritable or resentful; it does not rejoice at wrong, but
rejoices in the right. Love bears all things, believes all things,
hopes all things, endures all things. Love never ends.

Aristotle (384–322BC)
Love is composed of a single soul inhabiting two bodies.

The following quotations stress the importance of the friendship that remains after the first passion of love and that forms a sound base for a good marriage. A further selection of quotes and jokes suitable for use at weddings can be found in Chapter Eight.

Samuel Richardson
Love is a blazing, crackling green-wood flame, as much smoke as flame; friendship, married friendship particularly, is a steady, intense, comfortable fire. Love, in courtship is friendship in hope; in matrimony, friendship upon proof.

Martin Luther
There is no more lovely, friendly and charming relationship, communion or company than a good marriage.

Amy Bloom
Marriage is not a ritual or an end.
 It is a long, intricate,
 intimate dance together
 and nothing matters more
 than your own sense of balance
 and your choice of partner.

Speeches for other family occasions

Keep your speech simple, sincere, informative, entertaining and upbeat. If you want to make your speech amusing, don't go for too many laughs or you may be the object of them. Be honest and speak from the heart. If you feel very nervous, imagine you are in the informal atmosphere of a bar or restaurant, sharing a tale with friends. (See also pages 11 and 135 for advice on dealing with nerves.) Remember that the occasion is about the person being celebrated, and not about you. Whether for a life lived or an important milestone, those present want to join in the celebration. To some extent, you are their spokesperson, their voice.

Christenings and baptisms

Christenings or baptisms are religious services during which a child is introduced into the Christian church. These are usually important, meaningful occasions for family, friends and appointed godparents upon which the latter formally accept their role as spiritual mentors and answer for the child when he or she is too young to do so for him or herself. The ceremony can take place when the baby is very young, when the child is a toddler, teenager or even an adult, and, naturally, this will affect the content of your speech. Non-religious naming ceremonies are also held nowadays, but the following speech relates to a religious occasion.

Celebrations are often held after the ceremony, with speeches given by parents or godparents. If called upon to speak, consider your potential audience, which could range from the elderly to the newborn, including grandparents, uncles, aunts, parents, godparents, teenagers, children and babies. As with any speech, knowing one's audience is key to its success.

Father or mother of the child:

'I would like to thank you all for joining us to celebrate this wonderful and significant day. Today, Sarah was welcomed into the Christian church and community. The ceremony marked an important stage in her religious life, the first step on her spiritual journey. I would like to extend a special and very warm welcome to her godparents, who have so generously agreed to play their part in Sarah's spiritual upbringing. Those of us who are significantly older than Sarah will know that life is a journey punctuated by ups and downs. We know how much we value the opportunity to turn to those with greater experience for guidance, and I know that Sarah will appreciate the role that Jane, Amanda and Keith will play in her life in this regard. Sarah has already brought joy and meaning to our lives and we feel blessed to have her in our family. Please join me in wishing her a long, happy and equally blessed life.'

Confirmations

Confirmation is a Christian ceremony during which a baptised or christened person is admitted to full membership of the Church. It is seen as the fulfilment of baptism, when the person confirms the decisions made then on their behalf by their parents or godparents. The faith of the 'candidate' is strengthened or 'confirmed' by the ceremony, and each candidate has a sponsor, usually chosen from the baptismal godparents.

Celebrations usually take place after the ceremony, to which family, close friends, sponsors and godparents are invited. A speech should include thanks to all those who have played a part in the preparation for the day and in the upbringing of the candidate, and congratulations to the newly confirmed person and a toast to their future. Keep your speech both short and appropriate to the age group attending, which could range from grandparents to younger siblings. Beware embarrassing the young person who has been confirmed by focusing too much attention upon them, but you could discuss in advance if he or she might like to say a few words. It is a meaningful occasion and deserves to be treated as such by your speech, but an element of humour is also acceptable.

Speech by godparent or sponsor:

'Welcome everyone to today's celebration of Jack's confirmation ceremony. I would like to thank you for joining us on this special occasion, which marks an important milestone in Jack's spiritual journey and his journey into adulthood. Today, he chose to confirm his faith for himself, and I would like to thank Jack's godparents and sponsor for being here and for their invaluable contribution, care and love during his life. They were present all those years ago when he was christened/baptised and have helped guide him along the right path in the intervening period, generously offering their advice, support and sofas over the years. Today, they don't look at day older – in fact, you can see what they looked like from these christening photos I happen to have with me – whereas that little bundle of joy, tears and noise has transformed into the strapping young man we see before us. He is now a much bigger bundle of joy, tears and noise, but able to articulate those emotions much more comprehensively and comprehensibly.

I feel sure that Jack's godparents, sponsor and relatives feel as proud today as I do of how he has matured into such a confident, energetic, focused, happy and caring young man. Seeing him in the church today confirming his faith made me realize that he is now embarking on a new phase of his life, and I would like to ask you all to join me in wishing him great joy and happiness in his future. I am sure he will be turning to us and to his faith on that journey and would like to confirm that we will always be there for him. [*Pause*] To Jack!'

Bar and bat mitzvahs

Bar or bat mitzvah parties frequently feature many speeches – in both Orthodox and Reform circles there's nothing unusual in parents, grandparents, siblings, family friends and peers all standing up in turn and talking about the bar or bat mitzvah boy or girl, about their personalities, and anticipating what they will bring to their lives as Jewish adults. While bar mitzvahs for boys have been formally celebrated in the synagogue since medieval times, the bat mitzvah, or coming-of-age ceremony for a girl, is comparatively recent, and public bat mitzvah services and parties have only been commonly celebrated since the 1930s or '40s. In strict Orthodox communities, girls do not read in the synagogue, and the bat mitzvah remains a private party. Particularly moving speeches are often those given by the mother or grandmother of a bat mitzvah girl. Your speech should celebrate the special qualities of your bat mitzvah and welcome her into her new life as a Jewish adult: both a joyful and a serious moment as she fully joins the Jewish community. Many speeches address the bar or bat mitzvah boy or girl directly, then talk to the gathering as a whole. It is also common to celebrate, in addition, the family and the wider Jewish community.

Bat mitzvah
Speech from grandmother:

'Rachel, I remember your mother handing you to me as a tiny baby and inviting me to meet my new granddaughter. When I saw you wrapped in your mother's tallit [*prayer shawl, sometimes used symbolically at other key moments in life*] for the first time, I immediately felt a connection with you that remains as strong today as it was on that day over twelve years ago: a great joy in the new addition to our family and an intense curiosity to know who you would grow up to be.

Your bat mitzvah day is very special to you, and I felt so proud today as I listened to you recite the Torah and explain the interpretation you put on the passage. And it's very special for me, too: as a young girl in rather stricter times than these there was no formal ceremony when I became bat mitzvah – my coming of age was celebrated at home with just my immediate family around me. It was a wonderful, meaningful time for me, but I'm so happy that for you we can extend a more public, wider welcome as you make your debut as a Jewish adult.

Ladies and Gentlemen, friends and family, I've watched as Rachel has matured over the last year or two and admired her quick responsiveness to others. I've been touched by her imagination and the intelligence she's shown at our frequent Shabbat dinners when we've discussed serious issues, and her grandfather and I have often spoken of how much we look forward to watching her grow into the person we can already see her becoming. We've observed that she has already learned about the importance of having strong values in your life, and I'm excited and intrigued about the paths she will take as an adult. She will be supported by so much love from her family and from the great Jewish community she has grown up in, and today, as we celebrate her coming of age and entering that community, I'd like you to join me in wishing her the greatest joy in this new chapter of her life.'

Bar mitzvah

Speech by a member of the family or close friend:

'Ladies and gentlemen, today is the day that we celebrate David's coming of age in our Jewish community. The years of study that he has undertaken have culminated in the moving reading and Torah lesson he gave us in the synagogue and I'm sure that many people were as impressed as I was at the skill and self-possession he showed. Looking back (and it's quite a long way back!) to my own bar mitzvah I remember feeling more than a little daunted at the task of reading in front of so many people – but David, you certainly passed the test with flying colours!

In the family, you've been familiar as someone who is always active and on the go – the news I've had of you has often been of your achievements on the football pitch or at your school sports day. Your bar mitzvah today has shown a different side of you: a thoughtful and scholarly side that I'm sure we all feel privileged to have seen and shared in. Rabbi Siegel, with whom I studied all those years ago, used to say that a community is as strong as its youngest members, and I think that we should all feel joyful and optimistic about the strength of our community as you and your friends join us in it in this new chapter of your life.

Friends, I'd also like to use these few words to pay tribute to Ruth and Jonathan. They have been marvellous parents to David, and to Jackie and Reuben, also – warm, imaginative and loving. Those of us who are parents know that raising children is a tough job and the warmth of the family bond that Ruth and Jonathan have created is evident to all who have been privileged to be invited to their home. Bar mitzvah is a celebration of the family as well as the individual, so let us drink a toast to David, Ruth and Jonathan on this, David's very special day.'

Birthdays

Coming of age – 18th or 21st birthday

Although the age at which a person is considered an adult in the eyes of the law and society varies from country to country, state to state and between cultures and religions, the 'coming of age' birthday is normally one of the first great milestones to be celebrated. It is appropriate for a parent or guardian to mark the occasion with a few words.

The speech can be light-hearted or more serious, or a mixture of both, but its aim is to focus attention upon the birthday boy or girl and to make him or her feel special, highlighting both personality and achievements. If possible, select a number of memorable events to include in your speech. Humour is fine, but try to avoid embarrassing the boy or girl. Many young people have yet to develop their defence mechanisms and are easily embarrassed, particularly in front of their peers. Draw attention to their achievements and to the positive, commendable, admirable aspects of their personality. In order to present a rounded picture and to avoid falling into the 'proud parent or godparent/guardian' trap, you might want to include some things of which you are mildly and possibly humorously critical, such as spending too much time in the bathroom or expecting large gifts at birthdays. It's great anecdotal material, but make sure you don't cause either embarrassment or offence. If you are not a natural storyteller, make sure you rehearse this part of the speech or avoid it altogether.

The age, experiences and achievements of the person will dictate the nature and number of personal milestones that you choose to mention, but the following speech may form the basis of your own. Customize, expand, edit and build upon it.

'Good evening everyone. I would like to begin by thanking you all very much indeed for coming here to join Emily in celebrating her 18th [21st] birthday. Traditionally, this is the day you are granted the key to the door. However, these days the reality is that by the time you have reached the ripe old age of 18 [21], you will have had the key to the door for several years and lost it many times. Not to mention the key to the family car, the password to the computer, the control of the TV remote control and access to Mum/Dad's credit card.

On such occasions, as any parent or godparent knows, it seems like only yesterday when the beautiful 18- [21-] year-old before us was no more than a tiny, helpless creature, dependent on others for every need. To Emily, but not to us, it seems like an absolute eternity since she was struggling to get out of her buggy to walk by herself and refusing obstinately to eat her vegetables [or alternative hated foodstuff]. I feel it is my duty to warn you, Emily, that just as you have gone from babe-in-arms to young adult in the blink of an eye, the rest of your life will flash past with equal speed, so seize the day and live your dreams, starting now...

Many of you here today will know Emily very well, but others may not be so familiar with the details of the past 18 [21] years, of which I shall give a brief account. Trust me – it will be brief.' Now paint a picture of Emily and give a succint account of her life to date, describing her character and its development, important milestones and any memorable occasions. Pick occasions from the different stages of her life, researched with friends and family, to illustrate aspects of her personality. If you need visual help or props, look through family photos. You might want to make special reference to a family member who has had a special relationship with her, such as a grandmother or stepfather. Prompter questions include:

• What did she look like as a baby?

• Was she a happy, charming toddler or a difficult child?

• What were her first words?

• What was her first day at school like?

• What was her favourite food/pet/toy/holiday/games/TV programme?

• What were her best/worst moments in adolescence?

• What special moments did you share?

You continue:

'Now comes the part that will make Emily really squirm, and I promised not to do that. All children are very special to their parents, but I just want to explain to you why Emily is very special to us.'

Here you can list any achievements, academic, sporting, voluntary work etc. and emphasize personality traits, such as hardworking, kind, helpful, thoughtful, etc.

"It just leaves me to thank you all once again for coming today. Emily is lucky to have so many wonderful friends and such a supportive family. But most importantly, I would like to thank her personally for being such a truly wonderful [*god*]daughter, who has grown into a fine young woman. Will you please join me in wishing her all the very best for a long, happy and rewarding future. [*Toast*] Thank you very much everyone and I hope you will all enjoy the rest of the evening.'

Other significant birthdays

'Milestone birthdays' are causes for celebration, but may need handling with care. Not everyone relishes the idea of becoming a certain age, and although 70 is the new 60, and so on, it is worth checking how sensitive the birthday girl or boy is before you make repeated mention of their actual age. It might be better to refer to a 'distinguished' rather than 'venerable' or 'great' age, and try to use your speech to look forward to the life ahead as well as discussing the achievements of the past and the life already lived. As with most occasions, do your research about those likely to be present, as some guests may not have seen each other or the host for some time. Make sure you include everyone in your speech, perhaps making particular mention of those who have made a huge effort to be there. Try to leave everyone with a happy thought or memory of the day, especially the person whose birthday it is. A few lines from a well-loved poem or a favourite saying can form the perfect conclusion to a speech.

Speech by best friend for 70th, 80th or 90th birthday:

'First of all, I would like to extend the warmest of welcomes to all the friends and family of Edith who have made the journey to celebrate this memorable milestone, this important and very special day with her, despite slightly creaky joints and memories not being what they were. I was going to send out reminders, but then I forgot...

It is a wonderful achievement to reach such a distinguished age in such a distinguished style, to have lived such a full, rewarding and meaningful life and to have touched so many people in so many ways along that long and colourful journey. We are present to celebrate the past and to toast the future, to wish Edith many happy returns and a whole host of healthy and joyful years, full of wonderful experiences. If life begins as a blank canvas, then the one Edith has been working on is only partly finished. There are many more details to fill in, new horizons and landscapes to depict, different colour mixes to invent and experimental brush strokes to be made. Some of you here will know of Edith's great achievements, others may be surprised to discover just how many and varied they are. [*List here memorable events, projects or relationships.*] It is almost impossible to sum up a long life in a short sentence, but I shall do my best. To Edith, a true, trusted, loyal friend, a devoted grandmother, mother and aunt, a woman of the world and the century (20th and 21st) – a landmark in her own right, a national treasure and a great woman. Actually, that was quite a long sentence, but still...let's toast Edith! [*Pause*}
Happy 70th [80th/90th] birthday!'

Graduations

Graduation speeches provide the perfect opportunity for general celebration, specific congratulation and parental pride. Congratulations should be offered to the hardworking graduate, but beware embarrassing him or her too much by advertising achievements at length and harking back in too much detail to their academic or personal history. Parents, relatives or godparents delivering such a speech are allowed to be justifiably proud of the new graduate, but should keep the speech short and succinct, allowing everyone to get on with enjoying the occasion and offering their own personal congratulations. Remember, it is his or her day, not yours, however much support you provided over the years.

Speech from father to son:

'I would like to welcome you all to this splendid occasion, the culmination of years of sacrifice and dedication – Stephen's mostly, of course, but ours too... Seriously, though, today's graduation ceremony filled us all with pride. It's a day we shall never forget. What Stephen has achieved deserves a huge round of applause.

My family briefed me when I was planning my speech, and much emphasis seemed to be placed on the word 'brief' for some reason. So I shall limit myself to just a few minutes and then allow Stephen, BA Hons [*change where appropriate*] to speak for himself.

Being a practical man, I see my role as a father rather like that of a mechanic whose job is to equip his children with the right toolbox for life, to tell them about the practicalities, the pitfalls and the puncture remedies. My wife did a wonderful job providing Stephen with the emotional and spiritual fuel needed for his journey through life, and Nature added personality, courage and determination to the mix. Today, we see Stephen reach one of the milestones on that journey and would like to invite you to join us in celebrating it. To Stephen, the graduate!'

Speech from parent or godparent to son/daughter:

'Today is a wonderful day, a day that fills every parent, relative and friend of Sara's with enormous pride. It almost makes this parent speechless. So I shall borrow a few words from one of the greatest minds, Albert Einstein, instead. He memorably said: 'Learn from yesterday, live for today, hope for tomorrow. The important thing is to not stop questioning.' Sara graduated today after years of study, hard work and intellectual enquiry, supported by her own determination to succeed and to not stop questioning. In life, we never cease to learn, we never stop acquiring widom of different kinds and we should remember that there is always something new, different and challenging to discover.

Sara graduated today as a result of her own self-discipline, scholarship and sacrifices, all of which will equip her well for the next stage on her journey through life – that of work! But today, let's not think of that. Let's congratulate Sara on her achievements and allow her her moment in the sun, to relax and recuperate. As Einstein also said: 'If A equals success, then the formula is: A = X+Y+Z, X is work, Y is play. Z is keep your mouth shut.' Sara has done the work so let her play today and I shall keep my mouth shut once I have toasted Sara – the graduate!'

Reply by son:

'Thank you to all those who have joined me today to celebrate my graduation, and a special thank you to Dad for sticking to his brief! My own speech will be equally succinct, as I am keen to enjoy that pit stop on my journey through life that he mentioned.

But firstly and most importantly, I must thank my parents for all the support, guidance and love they have given me throughout my life, without which I would not be standing here today, sharing such a significant day with you all. Mum and Dad have always taught me to believe in myself, in my dreams and in the future. They showed me the importance of determining my own goals and working towards them. They helped me realize that life is full of ups and downs, victories and challenges and what I need to cope with both. They taught me the values of determination, discipline and hard work, but they always allowed me to dream my own dreams, one of which I am fulfilling today. I can't thank them both enough. To my parents!'

Anniversaries

Wedding anniversary speeches can be given by a number of people – close members of the family, the husband or wife, a close family friend, or even the original best man or bridesmaid. Such speeches are usually a happy, essentially light-hearted mix of nostalgia and humour, anecdote and congratulation. It is worth remembering that some guests may not have seen each other and/or the couple for some time and so try to include everyone in your speech, avoiding too many 'in jokes' or family references that others may not understand. Speeches can tie in the symbolic nature of the anniversary – golden, silver, diamond, ruby, etc. – and a short poem would be appropriate, even one composed by the speechmaker or jointly by the family. You could add extra humour by using old photographs as props, perhaps passed around by one of the youngest members of the family!

Golden wedding anniversary (50 years)
Toast to the couple by a close friend or original best man:
'Hello everyone and welcome to this very special day. It is lovely to see so many hale and hearty faces from the past, and to see all the friends, children, grandchildren and family gathered here to celebrate with Mike and Marion. *[Pause]*. Yesterday, I found myself wishing that life was more like it seems in films. And then I thought – if they gave Oscars for long-running marriages, I would be presenting one to Mike and Marion today *[possible prop?]*. Directors, producers, stars and gaffers (could somebody tell me what gaffers and grips do by the way?) of their own show, they have put on some wonderful performances, including all the different

genres – romance, comedy, tragedy, tragic-comedy, romantic comedy and even the odd horror movie and silent film! And Mike has pulled some stunts in his time and could have done with some more advice from the wardrobe department. But seriously, they have been professional, selfless, supportive, honest and sincere in their roles and relationship, unlike some stars of the screen we could name. And, as we know, 50 years proves too great a challenge for most film stars, and, indeed, royalty, but for Marion and Mike it has been a *Barefoot Walk in the Park* and today they find themselves *On Golden Pond*. They deserve every medal, Oscar and bouquet we can give them. To Mike and Marion – who will no doubt want to give a tearful acceptance speech thanking their family, children and everybody who knows them...'

Anniversary (can be adapted for number of years)
Toast to parents by son/daughter:

'On behalf of all my siblings, I would like to say a few words about our wonderful parents, Marion and Mike, without whom, of course, we would not be standing here. I was elected to speak on this, the occasion of their 40th wedding anniversary, being a man/woman of few words – so don't worry, this speech will be short, succinct and sweet. We will get to the champagne and canapés within five minutes! We decided to come up with four key words, all beginning with 's' to describe their marriage – one for each decade of their happy union. It was quite a challenge, since they have been such great parents and have been blessed with a strong marriage (there goes another 's' word) , but after much thought we chose the following: sacrifice, support, selflessness and security. Mum and Dad made many sacrifices for us throughout their lives and were always happy to do so. For that we would like to say thank you. We knew we could count on their support, whatever choices or decisions we made, however crazy, and they were there when things went right and when they went wrong. For that we are all deeply grateful. Selflessness is part of the job description for parents and they deserve promotion to Best Parents Ever for their dedication to us and to each other. For that we are eternally in their debt. And throughout our lives, they gave us the security that underpinned our confidence, happiness, independence and ability to go out into the big wide world and survive, knowing how much they loved us. For that we can only begin to thank them. That is what we would like to do today. So if you've all got a drink, let's raise our glasses and toast Marion and Mike, our wonderful parents. [*Pause*] Marion and Mike!'

Funerals

Writing a eulogy for a loved one can be one of the hardest things to contemplate. It can feel like a huge, almost overwhelming, responsibility, but reading the following advice could help you face the emotionally charged task with more confidence. The event may become less daunting if you think of your speech as a celebration of a life rather than a lament for its ending. It is important to focus on the life lived and the people touched by that life, including you. Every person, every life is unique and through your words you can express just how and fix a place for that person in the memories of all those at the funeral. Remember that you are surrounded by friends and family who want to hear and share what you have to say, not judge your speech. Breathe deeply before you start and speak from the heart. Talk to the person at the very back of the room in order to raise your voice to the right level. Think of this as a parting gift to the person, in all senses of the expression.

Try to sum up the person's character and personality, to bring them to life with your words, to show how they made a difference and to pay tribute to their talents and achievements and the way they lived their life. Ask friends for recollections and stories to include in your speech. Talk about the things and people the person loved and those he or she was loved by. Make people laugh, smile or even cry. You are bidding a final farewell to and summing up a life at the same time. You can mention their faults, weaknesses and difficulties, but do so with compassion and generosity of spirit. It is acceptable to discuss the person's less positive aspects – they are part of their make-up and life, but the general mood of your words should be positive and uplifting. Give those present something optimistic and memorable to take away with them and cherish. Talk about the person's legacies – their children, family, friends, projects and achievements, concrete or ideological.

Keep in your mind who will be listening to what you say. You may be revealing a fascinating side to the deceased about which they knew little. Share memories with those present, and don't feel embarrassed if you become emotional. Tears, yours and theirs, are a natural part of the healing process.

Don't speak for too long (five to ten minutes is fine) or the impact may be diluted. Rehearse your speech out loud a number of times, at least once in front of an audience – a member of the family or a friend – and be open to feedback. This exercise will give you an opportunity to time and fine tune your speech. Until the actual delivery, you may not realize just how emotional it will prove to be, so it is worth having someone to hand over to if you are unable to continue. Discuss this in advance with a close friend or member of the family – or even the vicar, priest or person officiating. Give your designated deputy a copy of the speech just in case you need to call on them to take over at the last minute or midway through your delivery. Make things easier for yourself by having your speech in large print or type with spaces between the lines for extra clarity.

Speech by a member of the family or a close friend:

'I would like to extend a very warm welcome to everyone here today. This is a very special, and emotional, occasion for us all. As the friends and family of Graham Smith, we have come to celebrate the place held in our hearts by a unique individual, to give thanks for a life that touched each of us in its own way and to pay tribute to a man we all feel privileged to have met and known as a grandfather, father, husband, son or colleague [*change as appropriate*]. Life is full of ironies and even the end of life seems to have its share. I was thinking this on my way here earlier, as I wondered which of you would come today. I realized that the person to whom we are bidding a very fond farewell is the one who would have loved to be here most. And even more ironically, how we wish he were! But in a way, and quite typically, Graham is still the life and soul of today's event. For it is his life and soul, his personality and achievements we are celebrating. It is hard to sum up a person and their journey in just a few minutes, and to help me do it I spoke to a number of Graham's friends and relatives and asked them to share with me some of the most precious moments they spent together. Some of you will know the occasions well, others will be new to the stories. What they reveal about Graham is his wonderful personality, his sense of humour, his consideration for others and his deep love of life. [*Specific personal anecdotes follow here*] And that was why I loved Graham while he was alive and why I shall continue to do so tomorrow, the next day and the next. I believe many of you will feel the same. So let us all say a final farewell in our hearts. Having wept for his parting, let us sing and celebrate the life that he lived.

Funeral readings

Poems and readings can be both succinct and meaningful and a favourite poem or few lines often form part of a eulogy. Ask friends and family if there was a special poem, poet or reading in the person's life or look at some of our suggestions below. Practise reading the poem out loud in private beforehand in order to become familiar with the rhythm, the pronunciation of all the words and their meaning.

Save Me
Psalm 69:1–3, 15–17, The Bible

Save me, O God: for the waters are come in even unto my soul.
I stick fast in the deep mire, where no ground is: I am come into deep waters, so that the floods run over me.
I am weary of crying; my throat is dry: my sight faileth me for waiting so long upon my God...
Take me out of the mire, that I sink not: O let me be delivered from them that hate me, and out of the deep waters.
Let not the water-flood drown me, neither let the deep swallow me up: and let not the pit shut her mouth upon me.
Hear me, O Lord, for thy loving-kindness is comfortable: turn thee unto me according to the multitude of thy mercies.

Other bible readings could include:

• Ecclesiastes 3:1–8 (King James version) 'To every thing there is a season'

• Ecclesiastes 12:1–7 (King James version) 'Remember now thy Creator in the days of thy youth'

- Psalm 23 'The Lord's My Shepherd'

- Psalm 121 'I will lift up Mine Eyes Unto the Hills'

Suggested poems:

The Tempest (Act IV, i)
William Shakespeare (1514–16)

Our revels now are ended. These our actors,
As I foretold you, were all spirits, and
Are melted into air, into thin air:
And, like the baseless fabric of this vision,
The cloud-capp'd towers, the gorgeous palaces,
The solemn temples, the great globe itself,
Yea, all which it inherit, shall dissolve,
And, like this insubstantial pageant faded,
Leave not a rack behind. We are such stuff
As dreams are made on: and our little life
Is rounded with a sleep.

Old Gaelic Blessing
Anonymous

May the road rise to meet you.
May the wind be always at your back.
May the sun shine warm upon your face.
May the rains fall softly upon your fields until we meet again.
May God hold you in the hollow of his hand.

From *The Prophet,* on pain
Kahlil Gibran (1883–1931)

Your pain is the breaking of the shell that encloses your
understanding.
Even as the stone of the fruit must break, that its heart may
stand in the sun, so must you know pain.
And could you keep your heart in wonder at the daily miracles of
your life, your pain would not seem less wondrous than your joy;
And you would accept the seasons of your heart, even as you
have always accepted the seasons that pass over your fields.
And you would watch with serenity through the winters of your grief.

Remember me when I am gone away'
Christina Rossetti (1830–94)

Remember me when I am gone away,
Gone far away into the silent land;
When you can no more hold me by the hand,
Nor I half turn to go, yet turning stay.
Remember me when no more day by day
You tell me of our future that you plann'd:
Only remember me you understand
It will be late to counsel then or pray.
Yet if you should forget me for a while
And afterwards remember, do not grieve:
For if the darkness and corruption leave
A vestige of the thoughts that once I had,
Better by far you should forget and smile
Than that you should remember and be sad.

Below is a list of other poems that would be appropriate, or have a look through the poetry anthologies listed in the bibliography (page XXX) for something that you like.

- ***My Life Closed Twice***
Emily Dickinson (1830–86)

- ***If I Should Go Before the Rest of You***
Joyce Grenfell (1910–79)

- ***Echo***
Christina Rossetti (1830–94)

- ***Do not stand...***
Mary Frye (1905–2004)

- ***Epitaph on a Child***
Thomas Gray (1716–71)

- ***Heaven-Haven***
Gerard Manley Hopkins (1844–89)

- ***Pied Beauty***
Gerard Manley Hopkins (1844–89)

- **'We Will Remember Them' (from *The Fallen*)**
Laurence Binyon (1869–1943)

- ***Requiem***
Robert Louis Stevenson (1850–94)

SUMMARY: TOP 10 TIPS FOR SPEECHES AT WEDDINGS AND OTHER FAMILY OCCASIONS

1. Research your audience and your material thoroughly, discussing both with the couple before the event.

2. Rehearse your material (and keep several copies of it about your person).

3. Remain sober until after your speech.

4. Relax (or at least try to look it...) and be yourself.

5. Keep your language positive, upbeat, inclusive and appropriately clean.

6. Use humour (and props) sparingly, but effectively.

7. Have some verbal parachutes or exit tactics for when/if jokes fall flat.

8. Start with a powerful first line to command attention and then maintain momentum.

9. Maintain eye contact with your audience.

10. Don't rush your speech but keep it brief – to your and their relief. It's all about timing and time.

speechmakers' bible

chapter 8

Jokes, comic stories and anecdotes

'A quotation in a speech, article or book is like a
rifle in the hands of an infantryman. It speaks
with authority.'
Brendan Francis Behan, 20th century
Irish playwright

This chapter will provide you with some of the content, reference material or raw materials for your speeches in the form of jokes, quotes, stories and anecdotes. Regardless of which you choose, it is vital that it is used properly and not just peppered into your speech. The following framework may help:

Item–Point–Relevance

Item: When using 'item–point–relevance', first we use the item, i.e. we tell the joke, recount the story or anecdote, show the picture or quote the quote.

Point: Often speakers are guilty of using quotes, humour stories, etc. without explaining why they are using them. For example, if a father was telling a story about his daughter's persistence in life in a father-of-the-bride speech it can often help to complete the circle by explaining the *point* of the story.

Relevance: Having told the story and/or explained the point, it may be necessary then to explain the relevance of that point within the overall context of the speech or to the audience who are listening to the speech.

An example:

Item
'Carl Jung said: 'The meeting of two personalities is like the contact of two chemical substances; if there is any reaction, both are transformed.' '

Point

'I believe the point that Jung was making was that when two people meet and connect, who they are changes forever as a result of that meeting.'

Relevance

'And when Chris and Sue met there was a reaction and both have been transformed forever. This fantastic transformation has managed to bring out the best in both of them as they are blooming with happiness, confidence and kindness.'

When using item–point–relevance, it is key that its use is not too structured and rigid and avoids the direct use of the three words. When used effectively this completes the circle of a good story by ensuring that the point you are making is clearly understood and the audience can see how it relates to your speech and the occasion overall.

Jokes and humour

Jokes and humour can also sometimes add to the interest and quality of your speeches. However, before embarking on using them you should apply the pre-joke checklist to avoid coming badly unstuck:

Are you funny/good at telling jokes? Beware of a difference between perception and reality. Just because you've been told you are a funny guy a couple of times does not mean you are a good joke teller. Get some feedback from a neutral, direct and candid person. If the answer's not a firm and immediate 'yes', then leave it out. For those of us that are not fantastic joke tellers, personal anecdotes or stories are often a far more appropriate solution.

Is this the right occasion to be telling a joke? Obviously, a funeral is frequently not the best place for humour. But even more mundane situations should be treated carefully with regard to humour. If a speaker is addressing a group of people who have under-performed or failed to deliver, it may deliver the message that what they are doing or have done is OK.

Is this joke appropriate for this audience? As mentioned above, sex, politics and religion are all sensitive subjects. This is not to say that jokes about them should never be used. The point is, is the joke appropriate for this audience? If in any doubt, take a representative member of the audience to one side and ask them for some honest feedback.

Is this the right moment of the speech for a joke? Humour has its place within speeches. It is often good as an engagement item near the beginning or during the main body. However, if you have spent time building up strong feelings and emotions in your audience by, for example, talking seriously about love at a wedding, you need to think carefully about then blowing this good work apart with a sledgehammer joke.

Is the joke actually funny? (to this audience) You must dry-run jokes with typical audience members. Just because it had your 20-something mates in stitches does not mean it will have the same effect upon an older audience. Sometimes the humour just won't translate.

Is the audience likely to have heard the joke before? Be careful about borrowing humour from popular media as it could well fall flat if everyone has heard it before.

Once you have ticked off this list, you then have licence to try to be funny, but how do you pull it off?

Entire books have been written on being funny and we won't attempt to replicate them here. Here are a few guidelines to jokes within speeches:

Focus on *how* you tell the joke: As Frank Carson says: 'It's the way I tell 'em.' Good delivery of jokes is a pre-requisite to telling them at all.

Timing: Never, ever rush the punch line.

Practise, practise and practise again: Just as with any rehearsal, knowing the joke inside out will free you up to focus on how you're delivering it.

Make it personal: Substitute audience members' names for the names of the people in the joke.

Concealed jokes: Try starting your joke in your normal speech style and audience members won't see it for what it is. Then when the light bulb comes on the impact is magnified.

Below are a short selection of jokes and amusing one-liners listed under theme and subject matter; they can be adapted, as necessary, for different occasions.

Age

My wild oats have turned into prunes and All Bran.

I finally got my head together; now my body is falling apart.

It is easier to get older than it is to get wiser.

These days, I spend a lot of time thinking about the hereafter... I go somewhere to get something and then wonder what I'm here after.

Birthdays

The only sure way to remember your wife's birthday is to forget it once.

When he lit all the candles on his birthday cake, three people collapsed from the heat.

Children

There's only one way I can make my children notice that I've got home from work – I walk in front of the television set.

Kids in the back seat cause accidents, but accidents in the back seat cause kids.

Christmas

Good King Wenceslas went into a well-known pizza parlour.
'The usual, sir?' said the waiter.
'Yes,' said Good King Wenceslas. 'Deep pan, crisp, and even.'

Cigarettes

I decided to give up cigarettes in two stages. First I'm going to give up smoking my cigarettes... and then I'll give up smoking other people's.

Corny

What do you call a mushroom that runs into a bar and buys a round of drinks for everyone?
I guess that would be a Fun Guy.

Drink

A glass of [wine/whisky/champagne] is said to cure all sorts of ills, such as the common cold. All you need is a candle and a bottle of [wine/whisky/champagne]. Light the candle, drink the first glass and wait five minutes. Drink another glass and wait, still watching the candle. Keep drinking until you see three candles, then snuff out the middle one and go to sleep.

A drunk was hauled into court.'Mister,' the judge began, 'you've been brought here for drinking.'
'Great,' the drunk exclaimed,'When do we get started?'

A drunk staggers into a Catholic church, enters a confessional box, sits down but says nothing. The priest coughs a few times to get his attention, but the drunk just sits there. Finally, the priest pounds three times on the wall. The drunk mumbles: 'Ain't no use knockin', there's no paper on this side either.'

Brenda O'Malley is home making dinner, as usual, when Tim Finnegan arrives at her door. 'Brenda, may I come in?' he asks. 'I've somethin' to tell ya.'
'Of course you can come in, you're always welcome, Tim. But where's my husband?'
'That's what I'm here to be tellin' ya, Brenda. There was an accident down at the Guinness brewery...'
'Oh, God no!' cries Brenda. 'Please don't tell me...'
'I must, Brenda. Your husband Seamus is dead and gone. I'm sorry.' Finally, she looks up at Tim.
'How did it happen, Tim?'
'It was terrible, Brenda. He fell into a vat of Guinness Stout and drowned.'
'Oh my dear Jesus! But you must tell me true, Tim. Did he at least go quickly?'
'Well, no Brenda... no. Fact is, he got out three times to have a pee.'

Exercise

The trouble with jogging is that by the time you realize you are not fit enough to do it, you've got a long walk home.

If God wanted me to touch my toes, he would have put them on my knees.

Golf

Two men were out golfing. As one was ready to take his shot, a funeral procession drove by the golf course. The man stopped what he was doing, put down his club, took off his hat and placed it over his heart. His partner was moved by this and said: 'That's the nicest thing I've ever seen you do!' The man looked back at him and said: 'Well, it's the least I could do after 20 years of marriage...'

Life

I started out with nothing, and I still have most of it.

All reports are in; life is now officially unfair.

If all is not lost, where is it?

Some days you're the dog; some days you're the tree.

It's hard to make a comeback when you haven't been anywhere.

The only time the world beats a path to your door is when you're in the bathroom.

When I'm finally holding all the cards, why does everyone decide to play chess?

Marriage

A little girl went to a wedding. Afterwards, she asked her mother why the bride changed her mind. 'What do you mean?' responded her mother. 'Well, she went down the aisle with one man, and came back with another.'

I like the story of the woman who had an artist paint a portrait of her covered with jewels. Her explanation:
'If I die and my husband remarries, I want his next wife to go crazy looking for the jewels.'

In the first year of marriage, the man speaks and the woman listens.
In the second year, the woman speaks and the man listens.
In the third year, they both speak and the neighbours listen.

The other day I overheard a woman telling her friend,
'It is I who made my husband a millionaire.'
'And what was he before you married him?' asked the friend.
The woman replied, 'A multi-millionaire'.

A best man's speech should be like a mini-skirt: short enough to be interesting, but long enough to cover the bare essentials.

One day a man inserted an advert in the local classifieds:
'Wife wanted'.
The next day he received a hundred letters. They all said the same thing: 'You can have mine.'

Money

Always borrow money from a pessimist. He won't expect to get it back.

I wish the buck stopped here; I sure could use a few...

It's not hard to meet expenses... they're everywhere.

Naughty

Sticks and stones may break my bones, but whips and chains excite me.

Opposite sex

Rules for finding a successful mate:
1. It is important to find a man who works around the house, occasionally cooks and cleans, and who has a job.
2. It is important to find a man who makes you laugh.
3. It is important to find a man who is dependable and doesn't lie.
4. It is important to find a man who worships your body.
5. It is vital that these four men never meet.

Politics

As Ronald Reagan said, politics is not a bad profession. If you succeed there are many rewards. If you disgrace yourself you can always write a book.

Speed

Every time I think the world is moving too fast, I go and queue up in the Post Office.

Telephone

Have you ever noticed that wrong numbers are never busy?

Stories and Anecdotes

As the saying goes, reality is often stranger, and funnier, than fiction. Whereas joke-telling relies to a certain extent on a degree of natural aptitude, most people are able to recount stories, either of events that have happened to them or to others. When combined with dynamic delivery, in terms of use of voice, facial expressions and body language, stories and anecdotes can be a lot funnier than jokes. An added advantage is that we find it a lot easier to recall and tell stories than we do to memorize and tell jokes, where we often trip over the punch line.

Although you can collect stories and anecdotes from reference books such as this, often the most effective ones are from your own experience. Ask yourself: 'What is the subject of this speech or presentation?' and then: 'What are some of my more memorable experiences with the subject of the speech?' These two simple questions will often unearth excellent and relevant stories. Here are some thought starters for personal stories:

Retirement: A story about you and the retiree.

Wedding: Stories about you and the bride/groom.

Business: Stories about joining the company/department.

Sales: Stories about you and customers.

Opening a new building: Stories about the old building.

Thank you: Examples of how you benefited from the person/their work.

Funeral: A story about you and the deceased.

Quotations

Quotations are another useful source of interesting content for speechmakers. They are effective since they can add impact and credibility to the point you are making, gain the audience's attention and sometimes make them laugh. Here are some key guidelines to help ensure that you use the right quote, at the right time, to the right audience:

Key guidelines:

Don't use too many quotes: You will lessen their impact and your speech will become mechanical

Limit them to one or two sentences: Audiences start switching off when they are read long quotes. Quotes are often most memorable when in a short, well-structured single sentence, e.g. *'I hear and I forget, I see and I remember, I do and I understand.'*

If you're not sure who said it, say so, but don't guess: Otherwise you risk undermining your entire speech. For example: *'Another form of reference material is statistics, but we must be careful with their use as we all recall the famous quote: 'There are three kinds of lies: lies, damned lies and statistics.'*

Make sure they are relevant: Just because you like a quote or think it is funny doesn't mean to say it will add to the effectiveness of your speech, it may just leave the audience wondering why on earth you have used it.

Libraries and bookshops will, of course, stock treasuries of quotations. Consider using quotes from well-known humorous writers such as James Thurber, Charles Dickens, Mark Twain or Oscar Wilde.

Songwriters are another good source of quotable lines. You can track down the words of songwriters from books or librettos or some CD sleeves. Good songwriters to quote include W.S. Gilbert, Sammy Cahn and Noel Coward. Alternatively, refer to a good dictionary of popular music.

American quotations can be found among the sayings of every president, while politics, business, morality and determination to win against the odds are popular subjects. Unless you are a great actor or orator, avoid any verse over four lines long. Five-line limericks, however, add humour, but be sure they are in good taste. Seek them out in a good poetry anthology.

Adapting quotations

The more you can relate your quotations to your audience and your subject matter, the more interested they will be. If the only quotation you can find is not very relevant or complimentary, adapt it. For example, at the wedding of a soldier you could start: 'According to the British Grenadiers, 'Some talk of Alexander, and some of Hercules, and others of Lysander and such great names as these.' But I would rather talk about Captain (groom's name).'

Below is a short selection of quotations.

Advice
Live within your means, even if you have to borrow money to do it. *Anonymous*

Age
You know you've reached middle age when your weight-lifting consists merely of standing up. *Bob Hope, 20th century American actor and comedian*

Wrinkles should merely indicate where smiles have been. *Mark Twain, 19th century American author and humorist*

Count your age with friends but not with years. *Anonymous*

Anger
Every minute you spend being angry with your partner is a waste of sixty seconds in which you could be enjoying yourselves. *Anonymous*

Animals
Outside of a dog, a book is a man's best friend. Inside a dog, it's too dark to read. *Groucho Marx, 20th century American actor and comedian*

When the mouse laughs at the cat, there is a hole nearby. *Nigerian proverb*

Appearance
If you actually like your passport photo you aren't well enough to travel. *Anonymous*

Confidence is that quiet, assured feeling you have just before you fall flat on your face. *Anonymous*

Babies
A baby is an alimentary canal with a loud voice at one end and no responsibility at the other. *Ronald Reagan, 20th century American President*

There are two things in this life for which we are never fully prepared: twins. *John Billings, 19th century American humorist*

Bachelors
Advice for those about to marry. Don't. *Punch magazine, 1845*

Children
Anybody who hates children and dogs can't be all bad. *W.C. Fields, 20th century American actor and comedian*

There is only one beautiful child in the world and every mother has it. *Stephen Leacock, 20th century Canadian author and humorist*

Exercise
Start slow and taper off. *Walt Stack, 20th century American senior-citizen marathon runner*

Kindness

You have it easily in your power to increase the sum total of this world's happiness. How? By giving a few words of sincere appreciation to someone who is lonely or discouraged. Perhaps you will forget tomorrow the kind words you say today, but the recipient may cherish them over a lifetime.
Dale Carnegie, 20th century American public speakier

Families

Important families are like potatoes. The best parts are underground. *Francis Bacon, 20th century British artist*

Health and wealth

I wish you health; I wish you wealth; I wish you gold in store; I wish you heaven when you die; what could I wish you more?
Anonymous

Never go to a doctor whose office plants have died.
Erma Bombeck, 20th century American humorist

Home

There is no place like home after the other places close.
Anonymous

Honesty

The best measurement of a man's honesty isn't his income tax return. It's the zero adjustment on his bathroom scales.
Arthur C. Clarke, 20th century English writer

Kindness
One of the most difficult things to give away is kindness – it is usually returned. *Anonymous*

Laziness
Anybody who isn't pulling his weight is probably pushing his luck. *Anonymous*

Life
Life is what happens to you when you're making other plans. *Robert Balzer*

Let the refining and improving of your own life keep you so busy that you have little time to criticize others. *H. Jackson Brown, American author of 'Life's Little Instruction Manual'*

If you can't convince them, confuse them. *Harry S. Truman, 33rd President of the USA*

Change before you have to. *Jack Welch, 20th century American author*

Losing
The only time losing is more fun than winning is when you're fighting temptation. *Tom Wilson, 20th century American actor, writer and comedian*

Love
Give her two red roses, each with a note. The first note says: 'For the woman I love', and the second: 'For my best friend.' *Anonymous*

Marriage

A good marriage is like a casserole, only those responsible for it really know what goes in it. *Anonymous*

Marriage resembles a pair of shears, so joined that they cannot be separated; often moving in opposite directions, yet always punishing any one who comes between them. *Sydney Smith, 19th century English preacher*

All marriages are happy. It's living together afterwards that is difficult. *Anonymous*

Every mother generally hopes that her daughter will snag a better husband than she managed to do...but she's certain that her boy will never get as great a wife as his father did. *Anonymous*

Marriage is like a violin. After the music is over, you still have the strings. *Anonymous*

Marriage is a great institution, but I'm not ready for an institution. *Mae West, 20th century American actress*

Better to have loved a short man than never to have loved a tall. *Anonymous*

An archaeologist is the best husband a woman can have; the older she gets the more interested he is in her. *Agatha Christie, 20th century English author*

Marriage is like a bank account. You put it in, you take it out, you lose interest. *Irwin Corey, 20th century American humorist*

Marriage is a matter of give and take, but so far I haven't been able to find anybody who'll take what I have to give. *Cass Daley, 20th century American comedienne*

Marriage is like a cage; one sees the birds outside desperate to get in; and those inside desperate to get out. *Michel de Montaigne, 16th century French writer*

I've been married so many times my certificate now reads: 'To whom it may concern.' *Mickey Rooney, 20th century American actor*

Public speaking
It usually takes me more than three weeks to prepare a good impromptu speech. *Mark Twain, 19th century American author and humorist*

Second marriage
I'm not so old, and not so plain, and I'm quite prepared to marry again. *W.S. Gilbert, 20th century English playwright and humorist*

Self-deprecating
I will try to follow the advice that a university president once gave a prospective commencement speaker. 'Think of yourself as the body at an Irish wake,' he said. 'They need you in order to have the party, but no-one expects you to say very much.' *Anthony Lake, 20th century US National Security advisor*

Success
If at first you don't succeed, try, try, a couple of times more.
Then quit: there's no sense in making a fool of yourself.
W.C. Fields, 20th century American actor and comedian

Temptation
It's hard to fight temptation. There is always the nagging
thought that it might not happen again. *Anonymous*

Toasts
A toast to sweethearts. May all sweethearts become married
couples and may all married couples remain sweethearts.
Anonymous

Here's to the bride and groom. May their happiness last
forever and may we be fortunate enough to continue being
part of it. *Anonymous*

The best cure for drunkenness is while sober to see a
drunken man. *Chinese proverb*

Deft Definitions

Definitions are very useful for inserting a little light relief into a speech. These are listed in subject order and are suitable for all types of speeches and presentations.

Adolescent
A teenager who acts like a baby when you don't treat him like an adult.

Adult
A person who has stopped growing at both ends and started growing in the middle.

Alarm clock
A device used to wake up people who don't have small children.

Amnesia
Condition that enables a woman, who has gone through labour, to have sex again.

Anatomy
Something everybody has – but it looks better on a girl.

Ant
A busy insect that still finds time to go to picnics.

Appetizers
Little things you keep eating until you've lost your appetite.

Bachelor
A man with no ties – except those that need washing.

A man who has faults he doesn't know about yet.

Book
An object used to pass time while waiting for the TV repairman.

Boss
Someone who is early when you are late and late when you are early.

Buffet
A French word which means: 'Get up and get it yourself.'

Careful driver
One who has just spotted the police speed trap.

Charisma
That mysterious something that fat, bald billionaires have.

Child
Someone who can wash his hands without getting the soap wet.

Cigarette
A fire at one end, a fool at the other and a bit of tobacco in between.

College

A place where some pursue learning and others learn pursuing.

Confused

Seeing your mother-in-law drive off a cliff in your new BMW.

Congratulations

Sugar-coated envy.

Conscience

The inner voice that warns us somebody is looking.

Consciousness

The annoying time between naps.

Cough

Something that you yourself can't help, but which everyone else does just to annoy you.

Courage

The art of being the only one who knows you're scared to death.

Credit card

What you use to buy today what you can't afford tomorrow while you're still paying for it yesterday.

Criminal

A bloke no different from the rest of us... except that he got caught.

Culture
A thin veneer easily soluble in alcohol.

Cynic
A man who looks down on people above him.

A man who regards getting engaged as a first step towards a divorce.

Dictionary
The only place where divorce comes before marriage.

Diet
A plan for putting off tomorrow what you put on today.

Discretion
Putting two and two together and keeping your mouth shut.

Divorce
Future tense of marriage.

Dumb waiter
One who asks if the kids would care to order dessert.

Duty
Something one looks forward to without pleasure, does with reluctance, and boasts about afterwards.

Earth
A minor planet with major problems.

Ecstasy
Discovering a second layer of chocolates under the first.

Eternity
The first 60 seconds of a blind date.

Etiquette
Knowing which finger to put in your mouth when you whistle for the waiter.

Expert
Someone who is called in at the last moment to share the blame.

Family
A group of people, no two of whom like their boiled eggs cooked the same way.

Fancy restaurant
One that serves cold soup on purpose.

Feedback
The inevitable result when a baby doesn't appreciate the strained carrots.

Free speech
Using someone else's telephone.

Frustration
Trying to find your glasses without your glasses.

Fungi
The life and soul of the party.

Gentleman
A man who holds the door open while his wife carries in the groceries.

Golf
A long walk punctuated by disappointments.

Gossip
The only thing that travels faster than e-mail.

The home
A place where a man can say what he likes – because no-one takes any notice of him anyway.

Husband
A man who wishes he had as much fun when he goes on business trips as his wife thinks he's having.

Influence
Something you think you have until you try to use it.

Intimidation
One mosquito in a large bedroom.

Key chain
A device that allows you to lose all your keys at the same time.

Leadership
The art of getting someone else to do something you want done because he wants to do it.

Manual
There are always three or more on a given item. One is on the shelf; someone has the others. The information you need is in the others.

Menu
A list of dishes the restaurant has just run out of.

Middle age
When knees buckle and belts don't.

Mobile phones
The only subject on which men boast about who's got the smallest.

Multitasking
Screwing up several things at once.

Office
A place where you can relax after your strenuous homelife.

Possibly
No in three syllables.

Prune
A plum that worried a lot.

Recession
A period when we have to go without things our grandparents never heard of.

Riding
The art of keeping the horse between you and the ground.

Road map
Something that tells a motorist everything he wants to know – except how to fold it up again.

School
A place where kids catch colds from each other so they can stay at home.

Semicolon
Half of a large intestine.

Semiconductors
Part-time band leaders.

Shin
A device for finding furniture in the dark.

Split second
The time between the lights changing and the driver behind you honking his horn.

Steering committee
Four people trying to park a car.

Tact
The ability to describe others as they see themselves.

Tomorrow
One of the greatest labour-saving devices of today.

Willpower
The ability to eat just one salted peanut.

speechmakers' bible

Index, bibliography and your notes

Index

Bibliography

'I have a dream' (pp87–91) © The Estate of Martin Luther King, Jr.

Every care has been taken to contact copyright holders. However, if any errors have been made we shall, if informed, make corrections in future editions.

Other speechmaking books

Complete Guide to Public Speaking, Jacey Lamerton, Collins, 2004
ISBN 0007165579

Public Speaking for Dummies, Malcom Kushner, Wiley Publishing Inc., 2004
ISBN 0764559540

Janner's Complete Speechmaker, Greville Janner, Thorogood, 2003
ISBN 185418217X

Lend Me Your Ears: All You Need to Know About Making Speeches and Presentations, Max Atkinson, Vermilion, 2004
ISBN 0091894794

Making presentations

Powerpoint for Dummies, Doug Lowe, Hungry Minds Inc, 2003
ISBN 0764539086

Beyond Bullet Points: Using Microsoft Powerpoint to Create Presentations That Inform, Motivate and Inspire, Cliff Atkinson, Microsoft Press, 2005
ISBN 0735620520

Poetry books

The Nation's Favourite Poems, BBC Books, 1996
ISBN 0563387823

The Nation's Favourite Love Poems, BBC Books, 1997
ISBN 056338378X

Poems to last a lifetime, Daisy Godwin (editor), Harper Collins, 2004
ISBN 0007177070

The Rattlebag, Seamus Heaney and Ted Hughes (editors), Faber & Faber, 2005
ISBN 0571225837

The Penguin Book of English Verse, Paul Keegan (Editor), Penguin, 2004
ISBN 0140424547

Quotations

The Oxford Dictionary of Quotations, Elizabeth Knowles (Editor) Oxford University Press, 2004
ISBN 0198607202

The Oxford Dictionary of Humorous Quotations, Ned Sherrin (Editor) Oxford University Press, 2004
ISBN 0198609205

Cassell's Humorous Quotations, Nigel Rees, Cassell Reference, 2003
ISBN 0304365882

The Penguin Dictionary of Modern Humorous Quotations, Fred Metcalf (Compiler), Penguin, 2002

www.quotegarden.com
www.quotationspage.com
www.worldofquotes.com286

Use these last few pages to make notes to help you with your
speech or presentation, such as any good tips, speeches or jokes
that you have heard recently.

_____

_____

_____

_____

_____

_____

_____

_____

_____

_____

_____

_____

_____